LEADING INDIANS TO JESUS

A PRACTICAL GUIDE

*From the experiences of disciples
making disciples in India*

Published by Abide Publishers
1600 N. Boonville, Suite B&C, Springfield, MO 65803

Cover design, typesetting, and interior design by Tyssul Patel.
hello@tyssul.co

ISBN: 978-1-952562-12-9

Printed in the United States of America

We are excited to be a part of your journey of learning how to walk alongside and share your faith with the Indians that the Lord has placed in your life. For those of us who have lived in India, we have worked hard to learn as much as possible about the Indian culture, adapting ourselves to better fit within the society. We understand that for those living in the States, this full immersion process is not possible.

With that in mind, we have created this book as a guide to both help you avoid some of the mistakes we have made, and to learn how to clearly and inoffensively share your faith with the wonderful people of India.

These are our stories and we pray that as you read, the Lord will speak to you of people in your life who you can be sharing with and that He will ignite within your mind creative ideas of how to build relationships using the gifts, talents, and abilities He has specifically given you.

In India, we live our lives under the idea of a Common Table. Meaning when we sit at our tables, be it to eat food, play games, or study the word of God, that we would have people who look, think, and believe differently than us there, and that there would always be a space available for one more person. Our hope is that by the time you finish this book, you will have the tools you need to start your own Common Table within your own home, and that the Lord will open your eyes to those around you whom He is inviting you to be part of their journey of knowing Jesus.

Your friends at the common table,

Live Dead India

In the beginning was the Word, and the Word was with God, and the Word was God. Through him all things were made; without him nothing was made that has been made. In him was life, and that life was the light of mankind. The light shines in the darkness, and the darkness has not overcome it. The Word became flesh and made his dwelling among us. We have seen his glory, the glory of the one and only Son, who came from the Father, full of grace and truth.

John 1:1, 3-5, 14

Contents

God's creation will be restored. People from every nation, tribe, and tongue will be redeemed. Together we will worship Him.

We are on that journey today as we partner with God to see this redemption story for India.

Jesus took a journey. The Word became flesh and moved into the neighborhood. He came and dwelt with us. He lived out the presence and glory of God among us, and we saw the goodness of the Father in Him.

As God sent Jesus, so is He sending us to live out the goodness of the Father in flesh and blood so all our Indian neighbors can taste and see.

When we talk about the country of India, we are talking about 1.4 billion people. That's a staggering number. In addition, there are 18 million Indians in the diaspora, Indians who are scattered all over the world from South Africa to Fiji to the United Kingdom.

Seven million people of Indian origin live in America today. There are 4.5 million U.S. citizens of Indian origin, which is about one percent of the U.S. population. There are also over 2.5 million Indian citizens living in America on business visas, green cards, student visas, etc. The second largest group of international students on American university campuses today is Indian (200,000 students).

So far, you have done the hardest thing it takes in reaching your Indian neighbor: caring and trying. You picked up this book because you care and are ready to try. Whenever the Lord sees a willing heart, He always makes a way. He will use you to see thousands of Indians around the world find hope and life in Jesus and to take that message back to their family and friends in India.

This is not a step-by-step guide. This book introduces you to some of the unique aspects of Indian culture—its religions, its worldviews, and its values—and starts you on your journey of connecting with Indians. It includes practical tips that you can use to better engage with Indians as you live life with them. It has starting points on how to contextualize the gospel for your Indian friend and how to disciple them on their journey to Jesus. Each chapter closes with meditative questions for you and your Indian friend.

This is not a guide to deconstruction. It is not about learning how to deconstruct any of the beliefs found among Indians in order to reconstruct their beliefs around the gospel. It is a book about the ways you can develop a deep, meaningful relationship with an Indian person that will spark their curiosity about Jesus. Your starting point is simply to allow your relationship with Jesus to guide you in your relationship with your Indian neighbors and friends.

This book only scratches the surface of Indians and Indian culture. It is impossible for us to uncover the totality of Indian life in a book of this size. So, don't be afraid to ask your Indian friends questions, and don't make any assumptions based on what you have heard in the past or even based on what you read in this book. If we are people who love God and His kingdom, we need to be people who love Indians and who learn how to engage with them.

PART ONE

THE UNIQUE ASPECTS OF INDIAN CULTURE

CHAPTER ONE

THE RELIGIONS OF INDIA

A young couple knocked on our door and asked to see our apartment. A surprising and strange request. As they walked around, I noticed that they both visibly noted my Bible on my desk. They then touched the Bible and touched their foreheads. They were not followers of Jesus, but they recognized the book as a sacred text and honored it as such.

India is one of the most religiously diverse and religiously attune countries in the world. The country is considered a religious melting pot of diverse religions. The majority of Indians are Hindu, and the largest minority group is Muslim.

Hinduism

Hinduism as a term was coined by descendants of the Persians, the Parsis, one of the founding Indian communities who were mispronouncing the name of the Indus River. The Persians called it the Hindus River and called the people who lived on the east side of the river Hindus. Their religion became known as Hinduism. In all ancient Indian texts, the religion is called *Sanatam Dharma*, which means eternal way or eternal duty or eternal path to god. The terms Hindu and Hinduism are never used in Hindu scriptures. The Indian people, because they are gracious, use our terms so that we can understand them better as a people.

Hinduism has thirty-three types of gods. You may also hear it said that Hinduism has thirty-three million gods. At the root of Hindu philosophy, though, there is only one god: Brahman. Brahman is the eternal origin or the cause and foundation of all existence. All other gods are considered manifestations of the one true spirit. Any god that a Hindu person worships is a manifestation of the eternal way. In fact, if one takes philosophical Hinduism to its extreme, the conclusion would be that there is no need to worship idols or recognize a multiplicity of gods because everything, including one's own self, emanates from the one spirit and is, therefore, god.

Within this eternal way are two major books: *Bhagavad Gita* and *Ramayana*.

The Bhagavad Gita is the philosophy of Hinduism. This short book contains the story of Arjuna, a king who amid war was visited by Krishna who comes as his charioteer and helps him understand what it means to follow god. This book lays out three paths of coming to god: *Karma Marg*, the path of duty, actions, rituals, sacrifice, and social obligations; *Jnana Marg*, the path of knowledge, meditation, yoga, and the study of scripture; and *Bhakti Marg*, the path of devotion and worship. The average Hindu is trying to follow and find god, and they do so by following as many paths as they can. They may focus on different means—rituals, meditation, prayer, worship, learning—but the end goal is a connection to god, to the one, to an understanding of who he is.

The Ramayana is an ancient storybook written by sage Vilmiki sometime between 500 to 100 B.C. It is filled with epic narratives and teachings on the goals for human life. It contains 24,000 verses, divided into seven sets called *kandas*. Among its many stories are the details of the journeys of Rama, an incarnation of Vishnu, god of protection. Vishnu is one of a trinity of the most important Hindu gods: Brahma the creator, Vishnu the protector, and Shiva the destroyer. Rama is the most widely worshipped Hindu deity, and the Ramayana shares his quest to rescue his beloved wife Sita from the clutches of Ravana with the help of an army of monkeys.

Islam

The Muslim religion in India has different facets. There are extremely religious Muslims and there are those who are heavily influenced by Indian culture and follow beliefs of folk Islam. Muslims believe in the God of Abraham, Allah (the Arabic word for god), and believe in the Old Testament and New Testament, which they call the *Kitab Mukados* and *Ingil Sharif* respectively. Central to their beliefs are the writings of their prophet Muhammad in the Quran and hadiths. Their belief is that in following Allah, they are directed by their prophet to live their lives based on good works, hoping that one day they will enter paradise because their good works outweigh their bad.

Culture and Religion Intertwine

There are many other religions found in India, including Buddhist, Sikh, Jain, and a limited number (in scope and scale) of Christians. It can be said with certainty that Indian people are on a spiritual quest in search of God.

In large part, Indian people are more impacted by their culture than by the orthodoxy of their religion.

I have seen instances in which my Muslim Indian neighbors seem to be more influenced by Hinduism than by Islam. I had been sharing the gospel with my Muslim friend, and one day as we sat together, a Hindu friend came up and mentioned that he was on his way to the temple with his parents. I asked my Muslim friend what he thought about that. He replied, "It's good! He is a good religious man and is following his religion." I then asked him, "But as a Muslim, do you think that he is in trouble or not going to heaven?" He simply replied, "His path is to be a Hindu, and he is following his path. My path is to be a Muslim, and I am following my path. Your path is to be a Christian, and you are following your path. We're all okay."

The friend's statement does not reflect orthodox Islam, but it does reflect orthodox Indian culture. That is what Indian culture values: following one's path to god.

QUESTIONS

What part of these religions make sense to you?
Which parts are more difficult to understand?

What stories in the Old Testament or New Testament
could be applicable to those from a Hindu background?
Muslim? Buddhist?

In what ways can you, as a follower of Jesus, become more
curious about other cultures?

CHAPTER TWO

UNDER-STANDING INDIAN WORLDVIEWS

Several friends did a "mini" pilgrimage when they were still Hindu. Someone encouraged them to ask Jesus about something, and when Jesus responded to them (as He does), their response to His response was to visit a church. On this pilgrimage to the church, they met Jesus (praise God!), but their motive for going was more cultural: Jesus did something for them, so they had to go see Him.

Indians hold a variety of worldviews. Those discussed here are more commonly held worldviews, but they are not held by everyone. Some are held by many Indians, while others are held by fewer Indians. The best way to know what your Indian friend believes is to ask them.

Pluralism

Pluralism is a commonly held worldview of Indian peoples from the *dharmic* tradition. This tradition includes Hinduism, Buddhism, Jainism, and Sikhism. Pluralism believes that all paths are equally valid and that all ways are equally good. An Indian of these traditions may defend their path to the death even as they defend another person's right to follow their religion.

> *I tell my male Indian friends that following Jesus is like entering a marriage. I ask them, "How would you feel if your wife said, 'I am happily married to you, but I am going to marry this other man as well.'" No Indian man would tolerate or accept his wife having multiple husbands. I tell my friends that Jesus feels the same way! If they are going to follow Him and be His disciple, He demands that they fully be His disciple. They cannot be His bride and the bride of someone else. Jesus demands this loyalty to Himself. But I also tell them that while they are on the journey, Jesus will welcome them to come to Him from wherever they are while they are making the decision to follow Him because He is good and loving.*

Your Indian friend may say to you, "Yes, I pray to Jesus, but I also pray to Ram." How might you respond to that statement? If Jesus is on their lists of gods, it does not mean they are a follower of Christ, but it does mean there is opportunity for Him to speak to your friend as they pray. Follow up a statement like this by encouraging your friend to continue to "taste and see that the Lord is good" (Psalm 34:8) and share with them that Jesus listens to everyone, no matter where they are in life.

When talking with your Indian friend, remember that convincing them of the truth is not your battle to fight. Simply allow Jesus to touch your friend's heart. You only need to present Jesus Christ as Lord. You will need to be honest with your friend, that when we follow Jesus, He demands that we follow only Him, just as the marriage illustration above suggests.

"Jesus answered, 'I am the way and the truth and the life. No one comes to the Father except through me'" (John 14:6). Pluralism hits up against the truth of the gospel, and this value among Indian peoples will be a barrier.

Karma

Indians are an auspicious sort, seeking a favorable outcome. Many revolve and measure a majority of their deeds around good and evil. Many Indians believe that everything they do matters and that everything they do sits on the scale of life. Good deeds and bad deeds are opposing weights on the scale and the balance between the two determines the outcome of their lives. Indians are raised with an awareness that when they do something wrong, they need to do something right in order to balance the scale. For example, you may invite them to church and because they did something bad that week, they will say, "Yes, I will go to church with you." They may not be interested in what happens at church; they simply want to balance a bad deed out with a good deed.

I was at dinner with one of my Hindu friends when she said that she had been bad that week so she could not eat meat that day. What she meant was that she had probably not gone to the temple enough that week or she had not prayed to the gods or she had been smoking cigarettes or she had been spending too much time with her boyfriend. She believed that she had done so many bad things that week that she needed to balance it out with good things before she could eat something like meat. It was a balance that she continuously lived in.

Indians of different faith backgrounds have an understanding that a much higher control speaks to the direction that their lives will go. This higher control goes beyond their own ability to control their lives.

Karma is a worldview that believes our lives are decided by our good and bad deeds, but it conflicts with Ephesians 2:8–9: "For it is by grace you have been saved, through faith—and this is not from yourselves, it is the gift of God—not by works, so that no one can boast." The Indian value of karma conflicts with the Kingdom value that says salvation is through the grace of God. Indian culture says that salvation comes through the good things people do by works, effort, and activities.

Years ago, I met a Muslim girl who was getting trafficked to the red-light district. I was so angry at this girl's mother because I knew that though she did not see what was clearly playing out in front of us, she was also not trying to figure it out. I asked her, "How could you send your daughter off with this man who says that he is doing one thing, but you have not verified it? You don't know this man and he could be lying to you." She simply replied, "I have to because that's what is written on her forehead." Meaning that this is what is supposed to happen to her daughter, so why would she check into it? Whatever is going to happen will happen and it has already been determined for this girl. What an excuse to just allow this to happen to your daughter.

Karma is a powerful idea that permeates so much of what they do. It is how they reconcile bad things that come into their lives. They just accept the decisions that are made. Going one step further, even though they call it fate, they still hold onto the feelings of jealousy and fear, and they still try to avoid bad things from happening.

We need to help our Indian friends enter the freedom of grace. We know this does not come by works or by how good we are, but by the grace of God who sent His Son to do something good, something that we could not do for ourselves, in order that we could enter His hope and life.

Reincarnation

The worldview of reincarnation believes that this life is not the end. Many of our Indian friends live with the sense that this life is just one of the lives on the journey. Hindus, Buddhists, Sikhs, and Jains see this life as but one of the stops along the way. They believe that if one has good karma in their previous life, then their *atmaa* (spirit) will get a better life the next time around, which is why karma plays an immense roll in a Hindu's life. They believe that if they do not get it right this time, they will have another chance the next time. We, as followers of Christ, live with the sense that we have this one life only. This life is our one opportunity, and we need to make the most of it.

> *Growing up, an elder told me that I did many good deeds and that's why I was born a human. If you do bad deeds in this world, in the next you will likely be born as an insect and then someone will trample you. My elder told me this right after I killed an insect.*

This idea of reincarnation comes up against Hebrews 9:27: "Just as people are destined to die once, and after that to face judgment." The clear word of God says that humanity has one life to live. We have one opportunity to live our life and make things right with God. There is no hope of coming back to try again. This life is the one opportunity to determine eternal destiny.

Remember you do not have to have all the answers. You do not have to refute all the issues. Sometimes it is enough to just listen. Sometimes the best response is to say nothing. You can return to conversations later when you have something to say.

I ran into a friend on an elevator. She is an OB-GYN trained in England. She told me that her sister recently had a baby and said, "It's so interesting. The baby was born the day after our father died. We look in the baby's eyes and we see our father. Since we know it is him, we are not mourning our father. We know that he has been reincarnated as this baby. My father was 30 years old when I met him when I was born, and now I had the opportunity to deliver him." I had no response so I simply listened.

Pilgrimage

Pilgrimage is the belief that persons should seek after god so that he or she can be found. In pilgrimage a god is not someone a person waits for; rather it is someone a person should seek. It is the idea that we should seek spiritual things.

India is in a constant state of pilgrimage. People go to holy sites and places throughout the year, to temples and famous shrines in the hills. Hindus will travel across India to visit the Ganges River *ghats* (riverfront steps) in Varanasi, sometimes as often as once ever year. Sikhs pilgrimage to the Golden Temple in Amritsar. Muslims hope to save enough money to one day make the journey to Mecca. Indians as a people are a people on the move; they are a people who are looking.

A good friend who is Muslim has a son who had a mental breakdown some years ago. We helped them get him to a psychiatrist who started him on medicine, and now he is doing great. In the process, she made the promise that she would do a pilgrimage to Ajmer Dargah, a holy site for Muslims and Hindus, as a thank you if Allah helped her son. It surprised us because during that time when we helped with her son and getting him to a doctor, we were very vocal about praying to Jesus and telling her that at times Jesus works miracles by way of medicine, and she sincerely agreed with us. It made us realize how ingrained this idea of pilgrimage is. When one is thankful, one responds with a pilgrimage.

This worldview among Indians offers great hope because Indians as a people are taught to be curious and to seek after spiritual experiences. As Hindus search, they talk to one another: "Have you found a god that heals? Have you found a god that blesses you? Can you tell me about that god?" They are a longing, curious people. Many Hindus have no problem doing Muslim pilgrimages in India and they have no problem visiting churches on Christmas to light a candle as a pilgrimage. They endorse that as a value. Muslims in India are more intentional in their beliefs. Where a Hindu would be more willing to attend and participate in other religious ceremonies, a Muslim will be supportive but content to watch from afar. Many Muslims are open and receptive to conversations about Jesus, though. The light of God still shines in India through this worldview, and the darkness has not overcome it.

Indians as a people are some of the easiest in the world to talk to about spiritual things. They are a hungry people that desire to know about God. The Bible gives us assurances about people who are seeking Him: "But if from there you seek the Lord your God, you will find him if you seek him with all your heart and with all your soul" (Deuteronomy 4:29); "you will seek me and find me when you seek me with all your heart" (Jeremiah 29:13); and "seek and you will find" (Matthew 7:7). This is the hope we have for the Indian people—they are a searching, longing people who are willing to take the journey with us.

> *There are not any temples near my home, but there is a beautiful tree across the street. A Muslim man had a vision under that tree and now this tree is developing as a Hindu shrine. There is always something going on there. Someone who felt like he had met with God dropped a seed and now all these other things are piling on top of it. Sometimes I feel like within the Jesus-following community we are less sensitive to the important places where God has met with us and with our families. The Old Testament is full of these stories of places where God met His people and they then piled up rocks as a memorial.*

This idea of pilgrimage is deeply ingrained in Indian peoples. Use this value for the kingdom of God. Engage your Indian friends in conversations about Christ. Ask them what they believe, so in turn you can share what you believe. Share your story with them. A wonderful thing about Indians who are pluralistic is that they are not breaking any law by praying to Jesus. They are not breaking any rules by tasting and seeing that He is good, so encourage them to seek Jesus and to pray to Him.

QUESTIONS

What are ways that you can share your beliefs based on the perceptions and beliefs of Indian peoples?

Write down a significant moment in your testimony that could become your pilgrimage to share with your Indian friend.

Reflections

CHAPTER THREE

APPRECIATING OUR DIFFERENCES

The value system of India and the value system of the West are vastly different, but that does not mean one is wrong and one is right. It simply means they are different. As you begin to engage with your Indian friend, you will find that you are often entering conversations from different viewpoints.

The best way to discover and know the values of your Indian friend is to simply sit and listen. Listen with the goal of trying to understand where your friend is coming from when they say things that are new to you. Become a learner. You need to know who your friend is in order to share Jesus from a perspective they understand and value.

I was talking with a girl who was planning to get married, and I asked, "Will you have kids right away, or will you wait?" She replied, "We would like to wait, but if my mother-in-law says that we must have kids right away, that's what we'll do." In that moment, everything American inside me thought, "If your mother-in-law tells you to have kids? It is your decision when to have kids." But I knew our cultures were different, so rather than responding, I felt like I was just supposed to listen. This was a moment I had to hide my "shocked face" and to show no reaction to what she said because that's not a wrong thing for her to think. We have to remember that our role with someone who comes from a different culture is not to make our culture theirs but for them to meet Jesus. Because I did not react and say, "That is a terrible way of thinking," and because I listened to understand and not to respond, we had many more conversations about Indian culture that we would never have had if I had tried to impose my American thinking on her. If you hear something that is different, you do not have to respond; just listen to understand.

This is incarnation: listening, learning, and living to understand another person. The word of God became flesh and dwelt among us. Jesus learned to eat Jewish food and learned to speak Hebrew and trained as a carpenter, so that when He spoke the word of God, He spoke it in such a way that a widow, a farmer, and a fisherman could understand. He could speak the Word and could share the truths of God in a way the people could understand because He had lived among them and learned.

God is calling us to dwell, just as the indwelling presence of the Spirit in us also desires to dwell in our Indian neighbors, classmates, and friends. We must learn about India and love India, because the more we learn about and love the country, the better we can communicate the gospel to the Indians around us.

As you listen to your friend, you may hear them talk about values and perspectives on the world that sound "weird." Remember these values and perspectives are not weird; they are simply different. It is of the utmost importance for us to learn and understand the culture of the people we aim to reach. Our learning and understanding offer us a grace that will enable us to impact the people around us. The values included here are just a sample of the cultural values held among Indian peoples. We have coupled them with the corresponding Western value for context, not for comparison. As we look at these values, we will also offer some ideas on how to engage in gospel conversations around them.

Religious Values

Honor and Righteousness

In the West we value righteousness. India values honor. Both can frame how we share the gospel with people, but honor will more deeply affect our Indian friends.

Righteousness is the idea that when we sin, we break the law. We have done what is wrong. We have done something that we should not have, and that's what hurts.

Breaking the law would not cause Indians to shrink back. Just because something is against the law would not stop them from doing it.

What would cause an Indian not do something is if it would bring dishonor on someone. The reason an Indian would not steal is because they do not want to get caught and bring dishonor on their family. They only want to bring honor to their family name.

We could preach the gospel to Indians as if they are from the West. We could tell them they should not sin because sin brings bad things their way. Sinning breaks the law and breaking the law has consequences. It is unrighteous to sin. But this idea of unrighteousness is not something that deeply affects Indians. Honor deeply affects them.

Scripture values both righteousness and honor, but we will focus on how Scripture values honor. "They did not honor him as God or give thanks to him," they "exchanged the glory of the immortal God for images resembling mortal man.... They exchanged the truth about God for a lie and worshiped and served the creature rather than the Creator," and "they did not see fit to acknowledge God" (Romans 1:21, 23, 25, 28 ESV). Here, Paul frames sin as the dishonoring of God, or when we sin, we dishonor God. When someone breaks God's command and lives a life contrary to Him, they bring dishonor to Him. This concept matters to Indians—they want to bring honor to their family and to their community and to God.

Paul defines the human problem of sin with reference to God's honor. Breaking God's law is just one expression of sin, but most fundamental to sin is the dishonoring of God. Yes, we should be righteous and follow God's law, but that is not the only thing. The dishonoring of God happens when we do not live a life that reflects who He is. When we live a life that does not reflect God, we bring dishonor to Him.

> When I am sharing the gospel with an Indian, rather than focusing on us as sinners in need of God's grace, I focus on the glory of God. I explain to them who Jesus is—the Creator of the universe, the perfect one, the sacrifice that gave His life, the Alpha and the Omega. He is the beginning of all wisdom. He is everything to us. As people understand who Christ is and the glory of who He is, a realization comes over them. They start to think, "Wow! I need to live a life that honors the one who created me in His image. I need to live a life to honor the one who created the universe."

Showing honor to God is a motivating value for Indians, so frame the gospel in a such way as to ask: How do we honor God?

Shame and Guilt

The West is a guilt culture. India is a shame culture. Righteousness leads to the emotion of guilt, while honor leads to the emotion of shame.

In the West, if someone sins, we say, "Don't you feel bad about that? That makes you look bad. Don't you know you're throwing your future away? This is going to get you into loads of trouble, and it's going to be bad."

In India, such logic does not work because the people are not individual or righteousness based. Guilt is not a driving force like shame is. To bring shame or dishonor upon oneself can also bring shame upon one's family and sometimes community. If you want to make an Indian child feel remorse, you say, "Don't you know what people will think about your mom and dad? If you act like this, people will think your entire family is bad. They will look down on your whole community because you are making everyone around you look bad. You better stop."

> When my dad finally figured out that I was not going to church to meet a friend but that I was going to church because I was following Jesus, he asked me, "Why are you going to church? A Hindu's son is going to church. What will people say? People will laugh." In his eyes this brought shame to the family. He believed that people would come to him and say, "Your son is going to church." To him it was shameful. It was something the family would need to hide, especially when it came time to find a marriage prospect for my sister because my going to church could be a downside for both families. In a Hindu community my decision does not only affect me, but it affects my sister.

God uses both guilt and shame. In the Bible God speaks about the guilt we have because we have sinned against Him. But the Bible also talks about shame: "You who boast in the law, do you dishonor God by breaking the law? As it is written: 'God's name is blasphemed among the Gentiles because of you'" (Romans 2:23–24). And "as it is written: 'See, I lay in Zion a stone that causes people to stumble and a rock that makes them fall, and the one who believes in him will never be put to shame'" (9:33). Our shame is dealt with in Christ; He came to take away our shame. God uses shame because we live our lives in such a way that God Himself is being looked down upon. These scriptures matter far more to Indians than guilt scriptures.

Indians may feel shame as they consider following Jesus. They may have questions like: What will happen if I do this thing and dishonor my family? What will people think about my community if I follow Jesus? We can tell them that Jesus came to take away their shame. He did not just come to take away their guilt, but He came to make them an honorable person and a right-standing person with Him and with the community around them.

How we frame the gospel matters. The words "you are guilty" are different than "you have sin." Guilt speaks of legal responsibility, while shame speaks of relationship. Shame is what comes through a breakdown of relationship. Both are truths in Scripture, but we need to remember who we are communicating with and who is listening. Indians live and think in terms of relationship and community, honor and shame, and it is important to present the gospel to them according to their values, in terms that their hearts understand.

Creation: Bad and Good

Indians, particularly Hindus, view creation as part of the illusion that keeps humanity away from god, and thus, creation is viewed as evil or bad. In the West, in our Judeo-Christian value, we see creation as good because God created the world, and He said it was good.

Taking your Indian friend back to the beginning, to creation in Genesis, is critical, especially for a Hindu. They believe the world is an illusion that keeps them from the reality of God, so their goal for life is to exit this world. There-fore, offering our friends eternal life is not something they are looking for. They are looking to escape this life and to be free from this circle that continues to go around and around.

Genesis chapters 1 to 3 are very foundational. I know that significant progress happens with some people after reading those chapters. Genesis makes a difference because they read the truth in the text. I have seen the change happen. In the Hindu worldview, the world is seen as an illusion with nothing good about the creation. This, then, becomes about a change in one's frame of reference. Sharing Genesis 1 to 3 reveals that there was a perfect world. An Indian's perspective begins to shift as the Word gives them a new lens to look at the world we are living in. It all starts to make more sense. The world begins to look like more than an illusion. The question then becomes: Is this world an illusion to escape or an orderly creation? It's like putting on eyeglasses. I put them on, and I can see the world so much more clearly. Some will read it and then think, "oh yeah, duh," because it becomes a no-brainer. They start to think, "Of course, this is how creation works."

The belief that this world is an illusion is contrary to the belief in a good, loving God who created a good world for us. Creation is a good thing that God created from His goodness. That is why Genesis 1 to 3 is such a key starting point. It brings understanding as to why war, famine, disease, and chaos exist in this world. The "in the beginning" sets a clear foundation of who God is and what creation is all about and who are we and how we arrived where we are today. From there, Christ begins to make more sense: Why did Jesus come? He came because this good, loving God who created us still longs to bring us back to Himself even though we walked away from Him.

Community Values

Community and Individuality

In the West we honor individuality and individual choice, rights, and freedom. In India, community is valued.

Philippians 2 holds Paul's thoughts on individuality versus community: "Do nothing out of selfish ambition or vain conceit. Rather, in humility value others above yourselves, not looking to your own interests but each of you to the interests of the others. In your relationships with one another, have the same mindset as Christ Jesus: Who, being in very nature God, did not consider equality with God something to be used to his own advantage; rather, he made himself nothing by taking the very nature of a servant, being made in human likeness. And being found in appearance as a man, he humbled himself by becoming obedient to death—even death on a cross" (vv. 3–8). Paul encouraged the community of God to lay down their individual freedom and rights and to think about others before themselves.

Indians look for this orientation towards community in other people. They look for people who will value others above themselves. They look for people that invite them to their house and make a meal for them when they are struggling. It means a great deal to Indians when you say, "We know your family has been struggling. Can we come pray for your family and sit with you tonight?"

> *When our gathering translates songs into the local language, any time the pronouns "I" or "me" are used in the lyrics, our Indian friends always translate them as "we" or "us." They have never thought of something as just "for them." They have always thought of things as for everyone.*

Indians are the type of community-minded people that show up at the hospital or send a note when they hear a mother or father is sick. They live this idea of being more interested in you than in themselves, of caring more about you than about themselves, and of putting your interests above their own. They will care about you as part of their community, not because of what you can do for them, but simply because you are part of their community. Indians look for people who will create community with them. Indians have an open home mindset. Anyone can drop by without a call or message and yet be warmly welcomed with snacks or even a meal. Though the Western mindset of a closed home is becoming more common in India, may it be up to us to always encourage an open home. An open home creates community and a safe haven for someone looking for a place to think or to be heard.

> *When we first arrived in India and our family was getting settled, different Indian women who lived near us asked if we needed help with anything. We politely let them know that we were okay and figuring things out slowly but getting things done. There were times when people asked for rides in our car (even when there were more people than seat belts) and we politely let them know that it wasn't possible for them to join us. We missed out on so many opportunities like these to help each other and live life together. I remember one time around Valentine's Day. For about 10 days, my husband and I were both sick and barely able to get out of bed. My kids, who were between the ages of 5 to 11, ate a tremendous amount of cereal that week because we were too sick to cook for them. But since Valentine's Day is special in our family, I pulled*

myself out of bed to put out a few candies, cards, and decorations for my kids. I have a picture from that day of my youngest daughter and it's obvious she had been spending a lot of time playing in the dirt while we were sick in bed. In the photo she is holding her card with a huge smile on her face and on top of her head is a huge bird's nest of hair that had probably not been brushed at all that week. Looking back, I wished I had reached out for help. Later, when I desperately needed help for something else, I gave in and asked our Indian friend for help. She turned to me and said, "Finally, we have all been waiting for the chance to help you!" From then on, our friendship grew tighter and stronger.

Those of us in the West who lean towards individualism may find it difficult to think in community terms. What would it mean to live with an open heart and open home? What would it mean to live incarnationally and invite Indians into your home or to visit your Indian neighbors and ask them to teach you to make tea or curry? Begin to develop a sense of community with them. Don't just live as individuals in a neighborhood. Start to live a joint life with them.

To the super strong individual, be vulnerable. Friendships are built by leaning on each other.

Relationship and Task

In the West we value tasks. In India relationships are valued, and as such, this may be a challenge.

In India our family made the decision to always put relationships before tasks. I don't have an office in India. Instead, I sit in the living room in my chair that faces the front door and do my work from there. Which means rarely do I accomplish any task in good time. Inevitably, while I'm doing a task—preparing a sermon, working on finances, sending emails—someone shows up at the door. In America, if someone shows up at the door unannounced, they broke a value of my culture: An uninvited guest has interrupted my work. As an American in America, I might scold my friend and say, "Man, why didn't you call first? You should have given me a heads-up and told me you were coming." But what is my response as an Indian? "This is wonderful! We were hoping you would come by!" Our guest will come in, and my wife, who was probably back in the home school room with the kids, will see them and say, "We were waiting on you!" And then she immediately starts making tea and we entertain our guests with gladness, not grumpiness.

Great responsibility and great blessing come with being in relationship with Indians. The great blessing is that any time of the day or night you can show up at their house and knock on the door, and they will answer with a "so glad you came!" The great responsibility comes when they knock on your door at 2 a.m. and you have to answer the door and say, "So glad you came! Please come in!" Then you welcome them in and make them a meal and meet whatever other needs they have.

I was at the train station at 3 a.m. once and my train was delayed. I called a friend and asked, "Do you know anyone in this town?" He said, "Yes, I have a friend who goes to the church there." So, I went to this friend's house at 3 a.m. and knocked on the door. He opened the door and looked at me, and I introduced myself and said my friend's name, and he replied, "Oh, so glad you came! Come in the house." He woke his wife and despite my protests, she kept saying, "No, we have to eat" as she made a meal and tea. Then they pulled their kids out of bed so I could sleep in their bed for two hours (again, despite my protests) before I returned to the train station.

Relationships before tasks, this how Jesus lived: "So they went away by themselves in a boat to a solitary place. But many who saw them leaving recognized them and ran on foot from all the towns and got there ahead of them. When Jesus landed and saw a large crowd, he had compassion on them, because they were like sheep without a shepherd. So he began teaching them many things" (Mark 6:32–34).

Things had been so busy for Jesus and the disciples, there was no time to eat or rest. Jesus turned to the Twelve and told them they were going to a quiet place to rest. The disciples got in a boat and set out, ready for a break. All the people saw them in the boat and said, "Looks like they are going to the other side of the lake," so they all ran around the lake and by the time the boat reached the other side, the people were there. The disciples were probably thinking, "We just wanted a break from you people and now we have to spend our vacation with you." So, they say to Jesus, "Lord, send them away. There is no food here and we're tired." Jesus' response? He had compassion for them. He taught and fed the people. Afterward,

He knew His disciples needed rest, so He put them back on the boat as He went to the mountaintop for the rest He needed with the Father.

It's not that Jesus did not get His rest. He just took care of all the others first.

In the West, we have goals or to-do lists that we hope to complete every day. When those get interrupted, we become frustrated because we know there is only so much time in a day to get things done. Others can then sense our frustration with their presence, and they feel unwelcome. The truth is, sometimes we need to put the task list down and focus on the person and the relationship being built right in front of us. Jesus is saying, "Relationship is more important than..." We have to ask, "Than what?" Relationships are more important than our time, rest, to-do list, work, etc.

If we will put others first and value relationships and the people around us, God will give us times of rest and refreshing. The refreshing comes when we put Him first and when we put our relationships before ourselves.

Harmony and Truth

In the West we value the truth. In India they value harmony. In India they don't want to hurt people's feelings. In the West we want to tell people the truth.

There was one week in which the theme of death rituals and the fear of death was circulating through the stories being told in the writers group that meets at my house. As others read, I remembered attending the funeral for a grandmother in the community and writing my reaction to what was happening. When my turn to share came, I pulled out this story and said to the group, "This is something I wrote in the middle of a death experience." I read about what I saw: a dog licking people's toes, and people sitting quietly while others wailed over the black painted coffin, and langurs (monkeys) jumping across the roof, and hail falling as the coffin was carried down a mountain to a hole that was half-full of ice. I read about how moved I was as I watched Hindu, Muslim, and Christian men lift and carry a coffin together to honor this mother and grandmother. I read about standing around the grave and hearing people repeating one Hindi word: jindagee (meaning life). This was a moment when I, as an outsider, was looking in and reacting to the things around me as I watched a whole community come around this family to comfort and love them. This was a moment of incarnation, sitting with a group of people and trying to understand and be like them. And I watched the reactions of those in the group as I shared because what I wrote about happened right there in India with Indian people. People sat and cried while I read. We then started to talk about what death is and how we feel about it. One young Christian lady from a Hindu background was sitting next to me. She has known the Lord for 10 years and tends to jump in and tell everyone what they should be feeling, so in this moment I grabbed her hand as if to say, "Don't say anything. Let's hear what they have to say about this." This was an opportunity for me as an American to sit in harmony rather than in truth. There comes a time for truth, but it might take a longer period of sitting in the tension between harmony and truth, waiting for that place of openness.

What does the Bible tell us: "Instead, speaking the truth in love, we will grow to become in every respect the mature body of him who is the head, that is, Christ" (Ephesians 4:15). We can do both. We can speak the truth of God in a loving way that does not destroy or breakdown another and in a way that does not divide us but brings us together.

Family Values

Decision Making: Family and Individual

Indians make decisions as a group while in the West we make decisions on an individual basis. For example, an Indian as an individual does not decide where to go to college; the family decides. It is about group decisions, not individual or personal decisions.

> *India has really rubbed off on my husband and me. We had a young lady on our team who decided to return home for a job. She said nothing about it during her decision-making process. She simply announced that it was happening. It surprised us. We thought, "Wait! We're your team. We're your family. We're supposed to make this choice together." We then understood what our Indian friends likely feel when someone in their community makes decision on their own without consulting someone in the community. It's such a beautiful way to make decisions in life. To have those people in your life that know you well and can speak into*

whatever decision you're making. It goes beyond who
you will marry. It includes daily life decisions, jobs, and
baby names. Pastors will often help in this process. It's
a blessing, honor, and privilege to have them involved.
There is value to community decision-making.

This value bears heavy on our Indian friends who are deciding to follow Jesus because everyone must face the cross and decide how it will come into their life. We in the West make choices for ourselves, but our Indian friends have more factors to consider when making decisions that will affect their family relationships. We have seen friends who went slowly as they waited for their parents to come along, but there came a point where they had to decide and say that they were going to follow Jesus.

Family Responsibility: Unconditional and Conditional

In the West our family responsibilities are conditional based on what the relationship is between family members. In India the responsibility to family is unconditional.

In our community we see an unconditional response
towards the family in the arranged marriages. Nearly all
marriages are here are arranged. The son or daughter
marries who they are told to marry with no questions
asked a majority of the time.

Marriage: Compatibility and Love

In the West we view marriage as a love covenant. It is something done with emotion; both people in the relationship must love the other. Marriage for Indians has more to do with compatibility. It is a family decision about two people coming together to raise a family, so the question of "who am I compatible with" is more important than "who do I love."

A young lady told me that her parents had chosen someone for her to marry, but she did not want to marry this person. If I was in America advising a 28-year-old woman, I would tell her that it was time for her to move out of her parents' house, establish herself in a career, open her own bank account, and keep building her relationship with her parents by visiting them regularly. I would tell her that it was time for her to become her own woman. But I could not say that to this young woman here in India. That would be terribly disrespectful to her and her family. Instead, I asked her questions like, "What do you want to do with your life? What are the most important relationships in your life? If you never spoke to your parents again, would that be okay with you? Are you willing for this to break relationships in your family?" She responded, "No, I don't want to do that." So, I asked her, "What are some ways through this?" I continued to ask her enough questions so that she could process and think about ways to approach the

> *situation with her parents. It's so easy for the Western*
> *mind to say, "Go out and prove yourself to your parents."*
> *But that's not helpful here in this culture.*

Oftentimes, Indian parents are looking for their son or daughter to marry "well," meaning that the spouse they agree to comes from a strong family background. Caste, religion, social status, and economic status can all play a major role in choosing a spouse. The spouse's education, appearance, and employment may also be considered.

Profession: Responsibility and Fulfillment

In the West we view professions as fulfillment. We want a certain job that gives us a sense of value and purpose. Indians see professions as responsibilities. They work a job to support their families and their mothers and fathers.

> *Recently, I met a Hindu husband and wife. The husband*
> *has worked away from his family for the last 10 years. He*
> *sees his family maybe once every year or so. I could not*
> *imagine how hard it would be to live away from one's*
> *spouse and kids all this time, but for him, men from his*
> *mountain villages have been working away from their*
> *families for generations. It was simply quite normal. It is also*
> *his way of showing love to his family. He lived sacrificially,*
> *so that his family was well provided for. Rather than his wife*
> *and kids talking about his absence as neglect, it was clear*
> *they saw that this was a way that he showed them love.*

Because Indians hold strongly to the value of taking care of their families, when the parents grow old, the children then have an obligation to take care of their parents by bringing them into their homes. In the West, we tend to make plans about which assisted living home we will place our parents in.

QUESTIONS

Building community begins with a sincere curiosity about another person. Questions about your friend's family are a good place to begin. What are some questions you can ask?

Sharing life with your friend is another big step in building community. What are some ways you can spend time with them?

Ask God how you can appreciate other people's differences more. Ask Him to use your curiosity about differences to bring you closer with Indians you know.

Reflections

CONNECT-ING WITH INDIANS

CHAPTER FOUR

THE VISION OF A COMMON TABLE

A shopkeeper who was a long-time friend of my team leaders inquired if someone could paint a sign for him. I could paint the sign (and did), but I could not accept payment because I was on a tourist visa. In lieu of payment, I asked if he could pay me with a meal because I knew his wife made the best biryani in town. As I became friends with the family, the shopkeeper asked if I, being a single girl in India, was ever lonely, especially around meals. I replied that it was hard sometimes because I come from a big family. He thought for a moment and then said, "Our family eats lunch together at this time every day. It's nothing fancy but come whenever you are lonely, and we will be your family." I have so many special memories of being with that family. There was no table. We sat on a mat on the floor and ate together. When my mom came to visit, they also hosted her. It was so beautiful to be invited into someone's home for meals.

We love Indians and we want Indians to know Jesus. We also love Afghanis, Somalis, and all God's people. God is bringing people from all over the world to Western shores, and that is beautiful. Many of these people share one trait—they are lost—and if there is anything that these people need, it is for the Word to become flesh and blood and to move into their neighborhoods. They need people who live out the gospel of Jesus Christ right where they live, work, and play.

John wrote in his Gospel: "The Word became flesh and blood, and moved into the neighborhood" (1:14 MSG). He also wrote in 1 John 1:3: "We proclaim to you what we have seen and heard, so that you also may have fellowship with us. And our fellowship is with the Father and with his Son, Jesus Christ." John's take-away of the John 1:14 truth, that flesh and blood moved in, is that we must bring people into fellowship with us so that they can enter fellowship with the Lord Jesus Christ.

We connect this world with the gospel of Jesus Christ by moving into their neighborhoods and inviting them into our homes. We can invite them to church or to an outreach, but more so we need to set a table for the lost. We need to make space for them in our lives. The gospel doesn't need more pulpits. The gospel needs more tables. The people of God must invite the lost into their spaces to share the gospel and their lives with the lost.

Relationship Around the Table

The Bible opens with people walking with God in a garden, and it ends with the tree of life in a garden that has living water flowing from it. We were made to walk in gardens with God. We were created for relationship with God. Jesus lives in us, so wherever we go, He goes with us. The God who lives in us walks with us everywhere we go. When we invite the lost into our space, we invite them into an encounter with God.

> When we first moved to India, our place was quite small. We had enough place settings and seats for four people, and our neighbors also only had space for four. Still, they invited us for dinner. They sat the four of us around the table and waited while we ate. We were eating by ourselves while they watched. We did

not speak much Hindi then and our neighbors did not speak much English. It was awkward. Before we shared meals at the table, the wife brought us a dish to our house. Someone gave me a heads-up to return the dish with food in it. I made macaroni and cheese, nothing amazing at all, and returned the dish to her. It was a great way to connect without a lot of language.

Theologian and author N. T. Wright said the gospel is this: God says, "I love you. I forgive you. Dinner's ready." I love you: God came down to this earth and dwelt among us. I forgive you: He died on the cross and paid the price for our sins. Dinner's ready: Jesus invites us to His table, to the wedding supper. That is the whole gospel of Jesus Christ: I love you. I forgive you. Dinner's ready. Jesus says, "Come in, and be a part of the family. Sit with Me, dine with Me, and enjoy My presence forever." This is what Christ invites us all to.

The greatest barrier to the gospel for our Indian friends is not theological. The greatest barrier to the gospel is not a Muslim sitting around and thinking that Muhammad is better than Jesus. The greatest barrier is not a Hindu sitting around thinking that Ram is better than Jesus. The greatest barriers are societal. They encompass identity and the question of who a person is. Most people are Muslims because their parents are. Most are Hindus because their parents are. They are not Muslim or Hindu because they went on a deep journey. They are Muslim and Hindu because of where they were born and to whom they were born.

This discussion about identity is important because those who are bought into their faiths with their identity will not be talked or preached into relationship with Christ. The only way they will enter relationship with Christ is to see a new society, a new identity, and a new people living out the gospel of Jesus Christ.

That's what the early church did. Acts 4:34 says that "there were no needy persons among them." No one considered any of their possessions as their own.

This was a community that lived out the ideal that they were the people of God and the family of God. They lived out their faith, and the people around them flocked to be part of it.

> When you sit at the table with Indians, you sit with the men and children. All the women are in the kitchen. My general rule is that the first time our friends invite us over for a meal, I let them honor us and I sit at the table with everyone. But the second time we visit, I will look for a way to the kitchen. I do not need to be at the table in conversation with men. They don't want me there, and I don't really want to be there. Let me be in the kitchen with the women. My go-to move is to pick up dishes and take them into the kitchen to make my transition. In America, we would say, "Women should not have to be in the kitchen. That's not fair." In India the kitchen is the table for women. They are not in the kitchen because they are not equal; they are in the kitchen because that is the table. We need to move with the culture because that is where our friends are.

The table designates a special relationship among those who sit around it together. A banquet was thrown for the returning prodigal son in Luke 15. Revelation 19 says that a banquet will be thrown for us.

In Scripture some of Christ's most powerful moments happened while sitting around a table. The Gospel of Luke alone mentions ten different occasions of Jesus' ministry being centered around a meal or a table: He shared meals at the houses of tax collectors Matthew and Zacchaeus (Luke 5 and 19); He was around a table when a woman anointed His feet (Luke 7); He blessed and shared five loaves and two fish (Luke 9); He enjoyed the hospitality of Martha and Mary (Luke 10);

67

He shared meals at the houses of Pharisees (Luke 11 and 14); and He ate with His disciples (Luke 22 and 24). The primary accusation Jewish leaders had against Jesus was that He ate with sinners. He welcomed them and sat with them. The table was open to the oppressed, the handicap, and the disenfranchised, and the tax collectors and sinners gathered around, leaving the Pharisees to question why He sat with them.

Overcoming Fear at the Table

Fear and anxiety are perhaps the first barriers you might find yourself having to overcome when eating at the table with your Indian friend. Hinduism, Islam, Jainism, and their diets are not things to fear.

We have no reason to fear what people do with their food. Paul said that whatever we eat or drink, do it for the glory of God (1 Corinthians 10:31). We are servants of the King of kings and Lord of lords. If a ceremony over food has taken place in our friends' houses, it will not affect us. We only need walk into a home with gladness and joy and eat what is set before us and enjoy life together with our Indian friends. We do not need to worry if there is a curse in the house because we are under the blood of Christ. If there is a curse, it cannot come near us. If someone else has prayed over a meal, do not worry about it. We can also pray over the meal and cover it in blessing.

We must overcome the kind of fear that kept the Pharisees from doing the work of the Lord. We must overcome any fear of association. We must never be afraid to engage with lost people. This is our calling, and Christ has given us the power for it.

One night we sat down for dinner with close Indian friends. We asked if it would be okay if we spoke a word of blessing over our food and for God to bless our time together because it was such a gift to have them with us. They readily agreed. After we said, "Amen," the wife of the couple enthusiastically offered for her husband to recite one of his mantras over us and the meal. Suddenly, fear overwhelmed me. I thought, "What spirit are we welcoming into our home with our children right here with us?" Reluctantly, we said yes. As he was chanting the tones were deep and loud. Our dining room suddenly felt like the inside of a temple. It was eerie for me. I spoke the name of Jesus over and over under my breath, anxiously waiting for the whole situation to be over. To our surprise, however, this couple asked us questions about being a "devotee to Jesus." Our willingness to be open to them led them to being incredibly open to us. We shared the whole gospel narrative with them in one night at that dinner table.

Where Do You Live

The first disciples of Christ were made as Jesus was walking down a road. Two disciples of John the Baptist heard John say, "Behold the Lamb of God" (John 1:36 NKJV). Those two turned and decided to follow Jesus. Jesus asked them, "What are you looking for?" Of all the questions they might have asked Him, they asked, "Where do you live?"

It seems like a strange question. Imagine you knew that Jesus was the Son of God. You just witnessed His baptism and heard the Father say, "This is My beloved Son, in whom I am well pleased" (Matthew 3:17 NKJV). Your own mentor just told you that here was the Lamb of God who will take away the world's sin, and the question you have is, "Where do you live"? They do not ask Him about creation or the end of the world. Instead, they ask Him about where He is living. The disciples indicated that they heard the news of the baptism, but what they really wanted to know was what Jesus' life looked like. They wanted to know how He treated His mother and His neighbors. Jesus responded, "Come and see." They spent the day in the house of Jesus, before one of them, Andrew, left and found his brother Simon and said, "We have found the Messiah."

> *I had a young man who came to the Lord and was a strong disciple, and I asked him what had the greatest impact on him making the decision to follow Christ. He told me that one day he was at our house, and he saw me walk up to my wife. He could tell that we were aggravated with each other about something, and we got into a discussion. He couldn't hear the conversation, but he saw all the facial expressions and hand waving. Then he said we walked away from each other, which he thought was very normal because he sees that in his society, so he did not think anything about it. But, he said, one minute later I walked back up to my wife and took her arm and looked her in the eyes and said, "I'm sorry. I was wrong. I got frustrated and I shouldn't have. It's my fault. Please forgive me." He watched me give her a hug and a kiss on the cheek. He said that was the*

> *moment he knew Jesus was real because he had never*
> *seen a man ask forgiveness of his wife. He had never*
> *seen brokenness before.*

When we invite people into our lives, it's not just to see how we do things right, but also to see how we handle things when we do something wrong, to see the good and bad times, to let people see what it looks like to be a follower of Jesus Christ.

One day spent in the home of Jesus changed everything. One day with an Indian in your life may change their life. One day of inviting them to your table may change everything. Invite people in so they can encounter the presence of Jesus Christ. The same presence that was at the table when Andrew sat with Jesus is at your table because Jesus is in you.

When we invite people to our table, we invite them to the table of Christ where they can experience His goodness. Jesus treated people incredibly. Just before His arrest in the garden, Judas Iscariot walked up to Jesus, and Jesus looked at him and said, "Friend, why have you come here?" He welcomed His persecutor. He welcomed His betrayer-friend. He opened the door for the worst offender. God has called us to be the kind of people that open our hearts and our doors to all the people around us.

QUESTIONS

Would you have allowed your friend to share mantras around your table? Why or why not? If not, how do we create a common table if we allow fear to overshadow the table?

What are some practical things you can do to make a meal for a friend from India comfortable?

What is something simple you can do to prepare your life and home to host people at your table?

Reflections

CHAPTER FIVE

EVANGELISM: WHAT IT IS AND IS NOT

I cannot talk with anyone for more than five minutes and not let them know I'm married because I love my wife so much. I can't sit with anyone for 10 minutes without them knowing I have three sons because I love my sons so much. My wife and my sons are so deeply a part of my life. And that's how it is with Jesus. In my first conversation with people, Jesus comes out because I value Him. I am not selling them Jesus. I am introducing them to my friend Jesus. Because they are my friend, I want them to meet my wife and Jesus. I want them to meet the most important ones in my life. I wish that everyone would follow Jesus, but I am not in friendship with someone because of the decisions they make.

"Evangelism" as a religious term in India and among Indians is a loaded term due to government restrictions and laws as well as the word's historical association with invaders and imperialists. The British empire facilitated a lot of mission work, which in the eyes of many Indians today makes Christianity appear invasive and imperialistic.

To us, evangelism means introducing a friend to someone who is important in your life.

> *When we talk about evangelism in our gatherings with new followers, we explain that it is our responsibility to simply introduce others to Jesus and that it is not our responsibility to change their minds or force anyone to think like us. We show them that our work is to present the truth of the gospel.*

Among Indians evangelism most often happens within relationships over time. Evangelism rarely happens in a moment of time with a decision made on the spot and it rarely happens through persuasion or dogma. In the West evangelism oftentimes happens in one conversation during which the gospel of Jesus is shared, a choice presented, a decision made, and a sinner's prayer prayed. That style of evangelism happens less often with our Indian friends.

When moving to India or connecting with Indians in America, we go with the mindset that we are looking for relationships, not for conversions. In reality, no one anywhere in the world can be forced to do or believe anything if the soil has not been prepared for the seed.

> *In ministry, there can be a pressure to perform and to win souls, which can sometimes supersede the gospel*

happening in a friend's life. When I first met my Indian friend, I told the Lord, "This girl is going to be my friend, not my project. I am going to be the best friend that I can be, but You have to do everything else. I will not force this." That prayer changed my whole outlook. This was the first time I switched my mindset, and the result was beautiful. It changed how I view ministry and discipleship. It was so simple, but so impactful. And Jesus did it! I have had more gospel conversations with her over teas and meals than any other friend. It took me a long time to get here, but I am glad. The Holy Spirit shows up when He is given space to do so; so often we take that from Him.

Relationship and friendship are a part of God's nature. God chooses to be in relationship and to have friendship with us. This is all in His nature. He created us for relationships, and He treats sinners as friends. Jesus calls us friends (John 15:14–15).

We are not talking about "friendship-evangelism" or "relationship-evangelism" when we talk about evangelism because relationships and friendships are not a means to an end. If they are a means to an end, they are not real, true friendships. We do not engage in friendship with our Indian neighbors simply to win them to Christ. We engage in friendship with our Indian neighbors because Jesus wants to be friends with our Indian neighbors. Even if they choose not to follow Him, we continue to be their friends because He still wants to be their friend.

And the motive behind our relationships matters. We are not Jesus salesmen. Our friends and the people around us can see through our motives. We must be people in relationship with Jesus Christ who introduce our friends to Jesus out of love for them, not from a desire to fit them into a new relationship that pays us a heavenly commission.

When Evangelism Isn't Always Quick

To be sure, there are times that a relationship does not appear to be leading to fruitfulness for the gospel, and we ask the question: Do we break off the relationship? Consider this: You can break off a relationship when Jesus breaks off His relationship with you. If Jesus ever decides that you mess up one too many times and gives up on you, then you can give up on someone else.

> I have been in relationship with someone that I thought was never going to follow Jesus. For over six years I shared the gospel with an older man, and for six years he showed zero interest. If I opened the Bible or talked about Jesus, he would leave the room or just tune out. But then one day he called me and said, "In my village we don't have a place where people worship Jesus like you do. Do you think it would be okay if I went and sat under a tree and talked to Him today?" I said, "Yes, absolutely, that would be great." He then said, "I have heard you sing songs. Do you think it would be okay if I just made up a song and sang it to Jesus?" I said, "Yes, I think that would be really good." This man would have been one of those that most of us, after a couple of years, would say, "I'm wasting my time," but today he is a very strong follower of Jesus Christ. You are never wasting your time when you are investing your life with people who need Jesus.

Don't fall into the trap of looking for "the easy ones." There are a lot of people that Jesus loves that will take a lot of time to come into the Kingdom. For our Indian friends, they need time to process the gospel. For them to follow Jesus may mean they lose their family or their job. It may mean they'll be cut off from their community. Oftentimes it takes years for them to process and to think about what it will mean to know Jesus. That is why friendship and relationship are important. We can walk with them through the process of their decision to follow Jesus, and it gives them room to process the gospel.

There was a lady known around town as being particularly nasty, dangerous for both locals and foreigners. I would not be surprised if loads of people have been kicked out of India because of her. If someone was speeding on her road, she called the police. If a streetlight was not working, she contacted the authorities. She wrote weekly complaint letters to...everyone. She was a brash busybody. I was told not to befriend her because it was better not to be on her radar. She decided she wanted to learn piano and my roommate began giving her private piano lessons. She wanted to learn "Amazing Grace," and as she did, she would stop in the middle of the song and say, "Did you feel that? Something just changed in this room. It feels different." My roommate always wondered, "Is she trying to trick me, or does she really feel something?" One day my roommate and I were out walking, and she pulled us into a shop. She began asking me questions about what I believe and wrote down notes in a little notebook that she always carried. When my roommate left India, this woman found me and insisted we be friends because she believed

I didn't have any. Then her mother became ill and was in the hospital. One of my friends stayed there with her for over a week. Her mom passed away, but in that time this woman decided she wanted to follow Jesus. No one saw it coming. All the sudden, she was telling the doctors to follow Jesus and calling all her friends and aggressively pushing the gospel on them. We had to slow her down and suggest she be gentle with her friends, as she had not appreciated aggressive pushes of the gospel message. She still has rough edges, but she is a changed woman learning about forgiveness and rebuilding burned bridges. And she still asks questions and writes answers down in her notebook as she processes all it means to follow Jesus.

Friendship and relationship help break down barriers of misunderstanding as many Hindus and Muslims in India and those that move to America have preconceived ideas about what Christians do and believe. As awkward as some of these conversations may be, they do break down barriers and stereotypes between friends.

People have visited my home in the evening and remarked, "Oh, you're not drinking liquor tonight?" Me: "I never drink it." Them: "I thought all Christians drink liquor to go to sleep." Me: "No, I never drink liquor." Them: "Oh, that's surprising, so maybe you're okay to be friends with." Some of my Muslim friends have even asked how many girlfriends I have. "I don't have any! I'm married and I love my wife," I answer. They often think that all Christian men have many girlfriends.

We threw a birthday party for our son. We were new to our community and invited our neighbors to come over. The party was going well. Everyone was playing games and having fun. A friend came up to tell me that the father of two brothers in our gathering had arrived. He was a conservative Muslim and religious person in the community. He arrived quite late and most of the food was gone, so my friend and I went to the kitchen to prepare a plate for him. As we did, he entered the house and proceeded to open every door in our place: cabinets, drawers, closets, the refrigerator. He was looking for haram (forbidden) things, like pork and alcohol. He fully expected to find them in the house. He eventually found a bottle of red wine vinegar and said, "Ah-ha!" I had to explain in my limited Bengali that it was not alcohol and that it was used for cooking, not drinking. I was not worried about his search because we had nothing to hide from him. Though, in fact, it was our German shepherd dog in my son's room that eventually ended his search. His sons had been part of our gatherings for some time but there was still the perception that we drank alcohol because we were Westerners.

There are many such misunderstandings, but to be fair we have similar misunderstandings about Hindus and Muslims and other religions. By spending time with people, we walk away with greater understanding and with the realization that they are just like us. For example, they love their kids and want the best for their family.

I started painting in a local shop, and the Muslim owner and I began to have lots of good conversations. One day, he began asking me questions about what I believed about religion and people being forced to believe one way or the other. I told him that I believed that if people have the freedom to choose what they would like to believe, that they will follow it more passionately and wholeheartedly than if they were told, "This is what you have to believe." He quietly thought about my words and then said, "Wait one second." He went and called for his daughter and told me, "I want you two to be friends." That began a year of a beautiful friendship between his daughter and me. We talked about our love of books and stories which often led to conversations of faith and what we believe. She then moved to a bigger city for college and every time that I went to that city, she and I would meet. On our first meet-up, she shared with me that her father doesn't like her to leave her campus but gave her special permission to meet me. She once told me, "I know you're Christian and follow Jesus. Before I came here, my father told me that he would give me full freedom to explore. Because of his family and where we live, he could never think about following Jesus, but he gave me the freedom to choose to follow Jesus. He

*gave me the freedom to follow my path." She and I had a
lot of conversations about faith and what we believe, all
with the blessing of her father.*

As you read these stories, you might be saying, "Muslims don't do that. They won't allow for such things." Muslims and Hindus and Buddhists are like you and me. They are lost people in need of Jesus, and they are searching for a path, and as we begin to share our lives with them, misunderstandings and misconceptions will begin to break down.

The Harvest Comes Through Relationship

The most fertile ground for sowing gospel seed is deep, meaningful relationships. Think for a moment about the parable of the sower, in which a farmer sows seed, and as he sows seed, some of it falls on the path, some on the stony ground, some on the thorns, and some on the good ground (Matthew 13:18–23).

The variable in this story is the relationship between the farmer and the soil. First, there is his relationship with the path. The farmer has not prepared the path for the seed. The hard ground of the path was not meant to receive seed so the enemy can come and snatch it away. Second is his relationship with the rocks. As the farmer prepared the soil in the field, he threw the rocks he found to the edge of the field. Some of the seed blew in the wind and landed among the rocks;

the farmer did not actually plant those seeds. He had no intention of having any relationship with those seeds in the stones. The third is his relationship with seeds planted and grown among thorns. The farmer tilled and prepared the ground and planted the seeds, but then he left, and weeds and thorns grew with the plants and choked the life from the plants. The farmer did not tend to that relationship; he let it go. Finally, there is the farmer with a deep, meaningful relationship with the soil. He tilled the ground and took the seed and put it in the ground. He covered the seed and watered it. He watched it and chased off animals and thieves. He waited for and received the harvest. The deeper the relationship between the farmer and the field, the greater the harvest.

We have to get down and get dirty if we are going to plant the seed and do what the Lord wants us to do with the gospel. The field and the dirt are incredibly precious because it is the place where the seed grows. On the one hand there is a recognition that you must get down in it and get messy for the seed to be planted, but on the other, there is incredible value in the earth, in the culture where the seed is planted. That's powerful for wherever we live in the world.

We can see a harvest through deep, meaningful relationships. When persecution comes, we can stand beside them and say, "We're with you." When the cares of this world come in and try to drag them away, we stand beside them and say, "Keep your eyes on Jesus. Keep your focus." If we are going to see a harvest with our Indian neighbors and friends, it will only happen with deep, meaningful relationships. It won't exclusively happen through campus ministry groups or in Sunday morning services, but it can happen when your neighbor can walk into your house every day to sit down and process the gospel with you. It can happen when they can see what Jesus has done in your life.

QUESTIONS

What relationships are you currently nurturing? If you currently have none, consider what relationships you could seek to develop.

What is God asking you to do to show His extravagant love to others?

Reflections

CHAPTER SIX

THE FOUR PRACTICES

As Westerners we tend to keep our distance and avoid talking to strangers. In general, we leave people alone. We like to organize and plan our lives, perhaps believing that if we have not invited and scheduled a visit with someone, then they should not come over and come in.

But when we decide to invite our Indian friends into our lives, we soon discover that our best laid plans and by-invitation-only policies become irrelevant. In fact, when they hear our offers of neighborliness and friendliness, they will likely come without an invitation.

And it is likely you feel completely unprepared for this, and that's fair. Let's explore four practices that you can start today to better engage and live out your relationships with your Indian friends.

Practice Hospitality

Romans 12:13 says "practice hospitality" and Hebrews 13:2 says, "Do not forget to show hospitality to strangers." Why do we practice hospitality? Because as Westerners we are not that good at it. We are good at taking care of ourselves, good at making just enough food for ourselves, and good at coming home after work and relaxing.

So if you want to be hospitable, you should practice, and you can start by inviting people into your life.

Hospitality is only hospitality if it is done with a cheerful heart. First Peter 4:9 says, "Offer hospitality to one another without grumbling." People notice when we do hospitality with grumbling. People know the difference between excited hospitality and grumbling hospitality.

> *One reason my wife's food tastes so good is because she is a great cook. Another reason my wife's food is so good is because she loves to cook. Love goes into every dish that she cooks. She enjoys it when people eat her food and are happy, and she loves seeing the smiles on people's faces.*

One challenge you may face as you invite your Indian friend into your life is the moment your friend comes by at an inopportune time. Such as, they worked all day and 9 p.m. is the first opportunity they have had free to visit. When you answer the door, your response should be a cheerful "I was hoping you would come to my house for a visit. Please come in! Let's eat together."

> *In India there is always food ready to put on the table. We keep snacks in the house and always have tea ready to put on the stove because we don't know when someone will show up.*

To practice hospitality, understanding a few simple things about your friend's habits and culture will go a long way at making them feel at home. Begin by stopping at an Indian market in your town and asking the manager or shop owner which sweet and salty snacks Indians love—then buy two bags of each. When someone visits make sure they have a drink with both their salty and sweet snacks. There is no need to ask your Indian friend if they want something because they will likely say no; just serve them something.

I thought I was so brilliant one time when I invited friends over. I had just received a package from my mom in the States. She sent me Country Time Lemonade, pretzels with the big salt on them, and Smarties candies. For my guests, I decided to make ice cold lemonade, put pretzels in one bowl, and unwrap the Smarties into another bowl with a serving spoon. When they came over, I served them some lemonade, which they took very small sips of. They never touched the pretzels, and they looked terrified at the Smarties. We had a great, though awkward, time, and I was not quite sure why. I mean, our kids ran up and ate the pretzels and Smarties, and my husband was downing the lemonade. As our friends left the husband asked my husband, "I just have one question: Why were you trying to feed us medicine tablets?" My husband was like, "What do you mean?" They thought the Smarties were medicine tablets. They had no idea what pretzels or Smarties were, and most Indians do not drink cold drinks. I was like, "Wow, I played that all wrong." Lesson learned, and now we know what snacks to have in our house.

Practice Neighborliness

What does it mean to be a good neighbor? Consider the story of the good Samaritan in Luke 10. It started with seeing. The Samaritan saw the beaten man. Being a good neighbor means we open our eyes.

> *People do not mow their lawns in India. Instead, a man*
> *with a very sharp knife comes along and cuts the grass, so*
> *Indians may not necessarily know what a lawn mower is.*
> *While we were back in America, we had Indian neighbors*
> *move in next door and they never mowed their lawn*
> *because, of course, they just didn't know how. I voluntarily*
> *mowed their lawn for a while and eventually my neighbor*
> *said with a laugh, "I should probably buy a lawn mower."*

After the Samaritan saw the man, he had pity on him. It is not enough to just see the need. We must have the compassionate heart of God. We must be moved with compassion to get involved. What we see must compel us to do something. The Samaritan was active: He bandaged the man's wounds and put oil on him and gave him wine, then he put him on his donkey and took him to an inn. We need to be the kind of people who see a need, are moved to compassion, and meet the need. We need to get involved in people's lives.

> *I know that when some Indian women come to America,
> they don't know how to drive. Being a good neighbor
> would just be asking, "I'm going to the grocery story. Can
> I buy you anything or would you like to come with me?"
> You could also offer to give them and their children a ride
> to the doctor.*

Finally, the Samaritan was committed. He saw it through. He had to leave but gave the innkeeper money to cover the costs and promised to pay the balance owed on his return. He was committed to the whole process of healing. When you do this, you convey to your neighbor that you are with them. We must be committed to being a good neighbor and walking with people in life.

> *During the pandemic I was stuck at my kids' house in D.C.
> for a while. Out of desperation I walked the neighborhood.
> I met so many Indians and Bangladeshis. On one walk I
> spoke three different languages as I asked people how
> they were and if anyone was sick in their house. People
> were open to those conversations. We have to be aware
> of who is around us.*

Practice Sharing the Truth in Love

Anyone using social media in recent years realizes that sharing the truth in love is more and more a rare thing. People may share the truth, but they may not do it with much love or compassion.

Our Indian friends need to hear the truth of the gospel of Jesus Christ, but they need to hear it from a heart of love and compassion. There is a difference between looking at someone and telling them straight that they are going to hell and looking at someone with tears in your eyes while telling them that Jesus came to die for them, so they don't have to go to hell. Those are different ways of sharing truth with people. We share God's truth in a manner of love.

At our business I share stories with everyone who is there. Then throughout the week, my goal is to visit with many of the women who were there and bring up the story that I shared that week in our conversation. One week, I shared the story of the resurrection. I went to one of the lady's homes and several other ladies were there, too. I noticed as we talked that they had been to vote in an election. They all had the black marker on their finger to signify that they had cast their vote. So, I asked them if they remembered the story about the mark on Jesus' hands. Some remembered, some didn't. As we talked through the story again, one lady looked at me and asked, "Why do you share these stories with us each week?" I had so much to say at that moment. I wanted to explain every detail of why the stories of Jesus are so important for our salvation. Instead, I felt a hesitation in my spirit, and I just simply asked, "Why? Do you not like them?" The lady's face looked shocked as she said, "No, that's not it. We all like them a lot. We just don't understand why you care so much to tell us about them. You talk about them all the time and we know it means a lot to you." I told her she was right, that the stories mean a lot to me because without Jesus I have no peace and I want that for everyone here, so why wouldn't I share these stories every chance I get? The ladies all smiled and then we discussed what true peace is. By simply asking that one question, it helped me better understand why she asked me her question. If I had jumped at the chance to share every detail about salvation, I would have missed the opportunity to have a deep conversation about fear and peace, which has ultimately led to many more conversations and to many of them understanding the truth.

Gentleness and kindness are mentioned more than boldness and courage in the Bible. We need to have boldness and courage in sharing the gospel, but more than that we need to have gentleness and kindness in sharing the gospel. We need the heart of Christ. Romans 2:4 says that God's kindness is intended to lead one to repentance. God does not hit us over the head with truth. He uses kindness to lead us to repentance. God also shares truth with us in love. Second Timothy 2:24 says, "The Lord's servant must not be quarrelsome." If someone wants to drag you into an argument, respond with "I am not here to argue with you. I am just here to tell you about the relationship I have with Jesus Christ." Focus on Jesus, not the argument. "The Lord's servant...must be kind to everyone..." (v. 24). We need to practice kindness and gentleness, and we need to practice sharing the truth in love through gentleness and kindness. "Opponents must be gently instructed" (v. 25). Seek the Lord for gentleness. Barriers are broken when we share the gospel in kindness and gentleness.

Practice Sharing Our Lives

"We cared for you. Because we loved you so much, we were delighted to share with you not only the gospel of God but our lives as well" (1 Thessalonians 2:8). Sharing the gospel is the easy part. Sharing your life is the difficult part.

> *One phrase we often use in our team is: The more uncomfortable we feel, the more comfortable they feel, and vice versa. Our goal is to be the ones who feel uncomfortable. That means we are probably doing something right.*

Learn to lay down your life, your wants, and your desires. Rather than reserving Saturday as "me time," join your Indian friend's cricket match, even if you don't know how to play. Change your date night plans and accept the invitation from your Indian friends to have dinner and spend time with them. When we get personally involved, it costs us time and energy, but our investment in these deep, meaningful relationships will see a harvest.

When my husband and I were living in Indianapolis, he was driving to the church in a blizzard. On an overpass near the church the wind was blowing fiercely, and he saw a man crouched down unable to move across the bridge because of the wind. He thought to himself, "No one from Indianapolis would be out in this weather." He stopped and offered the man a ride, which of course the man accepted. This man was Iranian and had recently won the visa lottery to bring his family to America. They were dropped into the middle of Indianapolis, and they knew nothing and no one. My husband drove him to this low-income housing by the church, and the man invited him up to the apartment to meet his wife and son. There was no furniture in the house and his wife was cooking over a one-burner stove, and she made tea for him, of course. This meeting led to a group of friends equipping that family with everything they needed, and in time they began to serve Jesus. Hospitality is not always practical and rarely fits with our plans. Hospitality like this is not really part of American culture.

Live with open homes and open lives. Open your life to the Indian people around you. Open your home to the lost. Let strangers come in and become family. Invite them to the table.

We had one young man who had been part of our gathering come under persecution from his family. He wasn't allowed to eat at his home, so he came and ate with us at mealtimes. This became a habit for a while until he was able to reconcile with his family. Although it was inconvenient to have to be home all the time to make sure he could eat, he has told us many times since then that he now understands the difference between how followers of Jesus love people and how others love people. He is still a strong believer today!

QUESTIONS

What is one way you can practice hospitality this week? Is there a snack you should add to your cabinet for your Indian friends when they visit?

If you were asked to share a story of Jesus, could you? Practice sharing stories around your table now so that it becomes natural when you invite others to your table.

Reflections

CHAPTER SEVEN

PRACTICAL WAYS TO PRACTICE

While in the States, we lived in a parsonage next door to a church. On one side of the church was a grassy area on a slight hill that extended out towards a major interstate. One Sunday evening we were getting in our car to leave the house when I saw a car pull into the church parking lot and over to the grassy area. Women wearing burkas got out of the car. I was confused and thought maybe I was just missing India. The sight was just so out of place. This Muslim family set up a picnic on this small hill. They laid out a blanket and started pouring tea for each other. I was sure they were lost. I walked over and greeted them. They poured me some tea and offered me some snacks and asked if there was a pond nearby (so maybe they were a little lost). I explained where the closest pond was and asked them what brought them to town. One of the girls was a student at the local university, and her family had come for two weeks to visit her. I asked her how her experience was and if she had many friends. She answered that she did not have many friends and she found the academic English difficult to understand. I offered to help her and welcomed her to our house to review her homework. That was all it took to start a relationship.

They come to us. They are our neighbors. You only have to open your eyes. There are numerous ways to practice hospitality and neighborliness, such as:

- Find a local cricket league.
- Invite Indian friends to birthday and anniversary parties.

- Frequently visit an Indian restaurant and befriend the owner or other customers.
- Locate a place where Indian students congregate on campus and join them.
- Welcome Indian friends into your home to practice hospitality whenever you can.
- Find neighborhoods where Indians live and walk in the parks.
- Befriend the priest at a local Hindu temple and get to know those who go there.
- Attend celebrations for Durga Puja and other Hindu holidays in local Indian neighborhoods and make friends there.

I have no idea how many Indians live in the Atlanta area, but I was driving around the city recently, and I passed a park that was filled with Indian people. There were so many that I think the whole population of Atlantan Indians might have been walking in the park enjoying the cool fall temperatures. Start going for walks in the park! Be aware of who is there and look for opportunities to join them.

Start a Conversation

Maybe you are wondering how to start a conversation when you are out. Much of it comes down to proximity. When we desire to meet Indians and we put ourselves in their proximity, Indians will often open the door for us because they are so relational. If you visit a park and see an Indian family sitting on a bench, sit on the bench next to them, smile, and say hello. They may happily start a conversation with you because they enjoy relationships. For those in school, when you see an Indian student with a chair open next to them, sit next to them. Sitting close to anyone is a great way of opening doors and having conversations.

> *Indians are very interested in our relationships, so I almost always talk about who I am, my wife, my kids, and the things I love. I also ask them about their family, their life, and what they enjoy. Most of my conversations are about them because I want to learn. As I learn about them and share about me, part of what flows out is always about Jesus. I can't have a conversation about me without having a conversation about Jesus because He is the center of my life. So, within moments of a conversation starting, I share my journey of how I came to Jesus and how it changed my life and how everything that I am today is because of Jesus. I don't want to meet somebody and a year later they find out I am married; that would not speak very highly about my relationship with my wife. I want people to know very quickly—this is who I am and who I am is because of Jesus.*

Do's and Dont's

- Do start the conversation as you would with anyone.

- Do ask their name and where they work.

- Do ask how they spend their time.

- Do ask how long they have lived in your city or state.

- Don't assume they are not from America.

- Do get a feel for the conversation. If you can tell they are from India, ask if they are of Indian origin.

- Do always ask if they have family in India and how they are doing.

- Do ask university students if they have family in India. Ask if it is hard to be far from them.

- Don't compliment their English. Most Indians have been speaking English since they were children. It is a national language in India.

- Don't assume they were born in India. They might be second or third generation Americans.

- Don't mention India. They might be from another South Asian country.

- Do avoid assumptive, stereotypical questions (i.e., why don't you eat meat?).

- Do avoid direct questions (i.e., why do you worship cows?).

- Do ask with curiosity and not judgment. Remember, just because it is different does not mean it is bad or worth judging.

- Don't be abrasive.

- Do watch your tone of voice.

Because I have lived in India so long, I love talking with Indians about India. I love talking about their home and places we have both visited. I love talking about Indian politics and cricket, and my wife loves talking about Bollywood movies.

Have a Meal Together

One way to welcome your Indian friend into your home is to share a meal together.

Do's and Dont's

- Do invite them over for a meal or cook a meal together.
- Do ask dietary preferences, then plan your meal accordingly.
- Do ask if they eat meat, egg, onion, and/or garlic.
- Do read labels for the above ingredients.
- Do have a new still-wrapped pan for cooking ready.
- Do explain that meat is in your home, but that you will not serve it.
- Don't talk about your love of beef or bacon.
- Do offer to make an American dish (with appropriate ingredients) at their house.

The first Indian family that I met and spent time with in America told me that pizza is the most international food. They order cheese pizza for any get-together with Americans. It's a good, safe, first meeting kind of food. It's also a good meal if you are not a good cook.

Visiting with Friends

Americans want to plan meetings and schedule get-togethers. Indians tend to have more fluidity in their schedules. You will know within the first few minutes if a person wants to have time for you, so do not operate out of fear and say nothing. Overcome relationship anxiety. People are quite forgiving when it comes to cultural matters because you are being kind and showing interest in getting to know them. In India, they offer us grace, so we expect it is the same for Indians in America.

I knew an Indian family whose door was always open. People were in and out all day long. It set a good example for us. A couple of generations lived in the house. The patriarch did not like being disturbed from 9 a.m. to 4 p.m. unless he planned it, but the house was still always open. It was okay to stop over. You just probably would not see him. You would see his sons or cousins for tea or lunch. To be sure, not every family is like that. You just have to learn through observation.

Do's and Dont's

- Do stop by and say hello.
- Do inquire about visiting hours.
- Do show interest in people.
- Do ask what they and their friend like to do together.
- Don't become paralyzed from saying anything.
- Don't be afraid of doing or saying the wrong thing.
- Do laugh at yourself and be willing to learn.

There is a gas station near our house that is run by an Indian family. My mom decided that she wanted to start a friendship with them. She told me, "I don't know what I'm doing, but I am going to try." She went there to buy some pizza and start a conversation while she was there. Then on Thanksgiving, she took plates of food to them. Except she didn't know that they didn't eat meat, so she went home and made plates without meat. That was followed by a gift from the family to her for Diwali (a festival of lights and one of the major festivals celebrated by Hindus, Buddhists, Jains, and Sikhs). A relationship started, and eventually they told her that they wanted to visit her. She said, "Sure!" But she had no idea what to do. She had no idea how to make chai and she had no Indian snacks, so she brought out hot tea bags and crackers on a plate. They didn't eat the crackers and they

politely dipped their tea bags, but it was all a little awkward.
They pushed through it even with a big language barrier.
For Mother's Day they gave her a gift and she returned
the favor. She has sat at their house and talked about her
chickens and the eggs they lay for her. The family is strict
vegetarian, but they all smile and are happy she is there.
The next week they wanted to come over and feed the
cows. It has been a slow relationship with many blunders,
but everyone is getting along nicely. My mom's story should
encourage those who don't know what to do. Just do your
best. Do something. It's okay.

If you are open to the opportunities, God will bring the opportunities into your life. Practice hospitality, neighborliness, sharing the truth in love, and sharing your life with your Indian friends, and Jesus will use you to connect Indians with you and your family, and with Him.

For some of you, the practical way to practice these things may be by moving to India. If you are committed to connecting with Indians, if you love Indian food and want to learn more about the beautiful country, move to India and be among them.

THOUGHTS

Brainstorm ideas of places you can visit in your community to meet Indians and practice neighborliness and/or write down thoughts that stick out to you from this chapter.

Reflections

PART THREE

CONTEXT-UALIZING THE GOSPEL TO INDIANS

CHAPTER EIGHT

CONTEXT-UALIZING THE GOSPEL

Often after working out at the gym, a group of us go get chai together. One morning as we sat with our chai, someone shared a story that reminded me of a proverb. I shared the proverb and talked about how my dad loved to read proverbs and tell us stories every night. It moved me to share funny proverbs to see if people could share stories to prove it true. It was so fun. They all thought "better to sleep in the corner of a roof than with a nagging wife" was hilarious because that sounds so eastern.

Before we contextualize the gospel, we need to de-contextualize the gospel. We are all followers of a contextualized gospel. When the gospel came to Western people, it was adapted from an Eastern thought religion to the sensibilities of a people who looked for rationality and reason to their faith. The early church, the first recipient of the gospel message, was not looking for rationality and reason, and yet this glorious gospel was adapted to the West so that we could understand and embrace the truth of Christ.

> *A friend of mine was on her journey to Jesus. She had already taken some steps, like when her family asked her to light the candles in front of the idols, she told them, "I would do it out of respect for you, but I need you to understand that I don't believe in this." They replied, "Oh, then you shouldn't do it." One day we were sitting together and talking about how people need to discern for themselves what they should or should not do in certain settings. We started reading through the story of Naaman, which is about this man who is sick and is told to wash in a river. His response was, "Why would I wash here? We have a holy river back home." She responded, "Like the Ganges!" It took us forever to get through the story because she kept interrupting and saying, "This sounds so much like India." I told her that the Bible was written in an Eastern context. She had no idea. So many of my Indian friends had no idea that the Bible was written in the East. They all thought it was a Western book. It helps to clear that point up with them.*

One challenge we have then is to realize that we are not contextualizing our Western rational gospel. Rather, we are looking to contextualize the gospel of the Bible. A Western contextualized gospel may not resonate with Indians. We must take the eternal truth of the word of God and present it in a way that Indian peoples can understand, embrace, and follow.

What Contextualization Requires

Contextualization requires that we have two great loves: love for God and love for our Indian neighbor. It requires we know the eternal word of God and it requires that we know the language and the culture of the people so that we can convey the truth in a language and by means that they will understand. It requires us to know the people with whom we are sharing in order to bring the weight of Scripture to bear on our audience.

Contextualization requires an intimate knowledge of the word of God. We cannot contextualize the word of God unless the word of God is deeply rooted in us. The word of God must be part of our daily life. We must be saturated in it. Before we frame the word of God for someone else, we must do our own thorough reading of the Bible. The great commandment says, "Love the Lord your God with all your heart and with all your soul and with all your mind" (Matthew 22:37). One of the greatest expressions of love is knowledge. What we love we want to know more about.

When I want to explain the gospel to an Indian friend, I will read through the Bible in six months. This gives me the full frame and narrative scope of the Bible. I make sure I know the Bible myself so that its truths are deeply rooted in me before I adapt (not change) the word of God for them.

We must have an intimate knowledge of our audience. The second command is like the first: "Love your neighbor as yourself" (v. 39). We need to know the people we are communicating with.

The first time I was called on to pray for someone in the community, I prayed in a way that was familiar to their Muslim background. I stood up, I took my shoes off, and I lifted my hands with my palms facing up. When I finished the prayer, those around me moved their hands over their faces as an act of receiving the blessing of the prayer. I prayed in a fashion that they recognized, and it lowered their defenses and made them curious. If I prayed in a way that was comfortable to me, it may not have made them curious. Fast forward, over a dozen years later, I was traveling with believers from a Muslim background from our gatherings. We stopped along the side of the road and played some volleyball with some other young men who were Hindus. I listened as one of the young believers started to share with these Hindu men and he changed all his words and spiritual terms to ones that are familiar

> *to Hindus. He got it instinctively. It's not about pretending*
> *to be a Muslim or a Hindu; it's about using the words and*
> *terms that best present the gospel to your hearers.*

We in the West might have it backwards. We spend four years in training centers and Bible schools preparing for a lifetime of ministry. Jesus spent 30 years sitting with fishermen. He spent 30 years working with carpenters. Jesus spent 30 years in the fields watching shepherds. Jesus spent 30 years gaining an intimate knowledge of Jewish culture and people, so that when He opened His mouth to express the kingdom of God there was a fluidity and naturalness to it. The socially lowest person knew exactly what Jesus was talking about because He took the eternal truths of God and placed them in a context that the Jewish people He lived among could understand.

There is no need to wait 30 years to share the gospel, though it is imperative to take the time to get to know the people around you and to intimately seek to understand them. The more you understand them, the more you can help them understand who God is.

How to Contextualize

Contextualizing the gospel is not changing the gospel. It is emphasizing the area of the gospel that makes the most sense to the Indian context. The gospel has a redemption narrative for rational, reason-oriented, legal minds like ours, but the same gospel has redemptive narrative for people from a relational background.

Contextualization simply means that we have a different starting point when we share the gospel message with our Indian friends. We are not changing the message. We choose words that best help them understand the good news we are sharing with them. We find a pathway or connection point that they understand and that leads them to the gospel. The starting point is rarely, "Jesus is God's Son, and you cannot worship idols." Perhaps there is a time for that starting point, but often the journey starts elsewhere in God's word.

> A guy who came to faith in our community also helps at the business. He and I were in a room at the business, when one of the ladies came in. My back was to them as she asked him about what we do on Friday nights. "What an interesting question," I thought. I listened as he gave a basic overview of our gathering. He then asked her if she ever heard of Jesus. "No, never," she responded. He went on to tell her a string of Jesus' miracle stories. I had never heard him verbalize all of that to someone else. It was a powerful moment. He was able to say things in a way that this woman understood and in a way that painted a clear picture. After she left the room, I turned around and said to him, "That was such a great job. You really knew those stories." He replied, "Auntie, I know I could have told her a lot more, but I was just giving her a little bit. We live close to each other, and when she has more questions, she will come ask me and I will tell her more." He then said, "You can't give it all to them at once." I said, "Yes, you're right." He never realized that was exactly what we did with him. No one told him to share that way. He just recognized, even in his infant stage of walking with Jesus, to trust and

> *be sensitive to the Holy Spirit. It is not our job to coerce*
> *or convince anyone. We just need to share the good news*
> *that then becomes good news for others.*

Know the word of God and know your friend. Allow yourself to be a good news bearer by simply sharing a story that connects with your Indian friend. Be in tune with the Holy Spirit and allow Him to create a sense of curiosity in your friend as they consider Jesus for what might be the very first time. We Westerners may be used to sharing the Romans Road with our unbelieving friends, and we want to share every part of the gospel from the beginning. Do not feel as if you are deceiving anyone if they do not hear the full message in the first conversation. We can start with a portion and allow our friends to "taste and see." We can see what their response is and build on that.

> *It's taste and see, not gorge and see. We are not shoving*
> *a buffet down someone's throat. We are giving them the*
> *good news, not delivering a death sentence. Allow the*
> *Lord to gently guide.*

Four Starting Points

Let's look at four Eastern perspectives that you can keep in mind when you share Jesus as a Westerner.

1 *"I make decisions alongside my community."*

Start from the perspective that your friend is an individual in a community, not an individual apart from their community. This is about a whole family or community, not just one person. Consider Lydia and the Philippian jailer in Acts 16—their entire households were saved and baptized. Community decisions were made!

Look for your Indian friends to process with their family. The whole community may not decide to follow Jesus, but they will be a part of your friend's process. And that's key. When your friend makes the decision, it will have been in the normal context of their community. Encourage your friend to think outwardly; what does Jesus want to do through them for their community.

What to say to your Indian friend:

"Jesus did not come to pull you away from your family. He is revealing Himself to you because He loves your family and wants all of them to come into a relationship with Him. Jesus wants to use you as the first fruits to reveal His light to your family and community."

2 *"When my community isn't in agreement with my decisions, I feel shame."*

Guilt is an individual feeling. Shame is a community feeling, and Indians as a community-oriented people are more attune to shame than guilt.

What to say to your Indian friend:

"You were created by God. Your actions will either honor Him as King or shame Him. The way you live your life is not just a reflection on you but on the God who created you. That is the reason why we stay away from sin and why we live a life of kindness, peace, and honor. That is why we forgive. We want people to see Christ in us."

3 *"I have been seeking a reconciled relationship with God."*

Redemption is a legal transaction: you owed something legally and someone paid the price to remove the debt from your life. Much of our Western gospel presentation is redemption oriented.

But reconciliation is about relationship, about coming into a right relationship with God. Indians are more in tune with relational reality. They want to connect and be one with God.

What to say to your Indian friend:

"Do you feel connected to God? Do you want a relationship with God? Are you looking for God? God knew we were searching and longing for a relationship with Him. Jesus came to bring you into right relationship with God. We once lived in a garden with God, but our sin separated us. Jesus came to restore us back into relationship so we can walk with God again."

4   "If I follow Jesus, do I have to use your symbols and look like you?"

Do you know what an Indian wedding looks like, or what color they wear in mourning, or how they worship? Do you know the meanings behind the symbols found in their ceremonies?

Understanding the meanings beyond our symbols and their symbols may offer starting points in sharing the gospel. The list below can get you started:

	In the West	In the East
Wedding	White wedding dress Rings exchanged Stand in front of an altar	Red sari Mangalsutra (necklace) Walk around the flame
Mourning	Black clothes	Colorful clothes Widows wear white
Worship	Sit in a chair Wear shoes Bible on the floor	Sit on the floor Remove shoes Bible elevated in respect

What to say to your Indian friend:

"Following Jesus doesn't mean abandoning your heritage and culture. Let's explore how Jesus can abide with you in your current cultural and worship practices."

QUESTIONS

What ways have you contextualized the Bible in your own life and culture? As you now learn about India, what are some stories of the Bible that you can now see how to contextualize for Indians?

What does your own time with the Lord look like? Are there ways that you feel the Lord asking you to go deeper in your own walk with Him?

Reflections

CHAPTER NINE

HELPING YOUR FRIEND CONTEXT-UALIZE

I would not go to a village where all the people were starving to death, erect a fence, put all the food on the outside of the fence, and then give a lecture on the nutritious value of food. Rather, I would immediately give them the food, and when their body was more whole and healthier, I would explain the nutritious value of food and what they can do to stay whole and not become sick. We don't have to lecture about the goodness of God. They can experience the goodness of God. We can give that freely and explain as we go.

We do not want to make life difficult for our friends as they journey towards Jesus. Contextualization will help our Indian friends make biblical, Christ-honoring, family-affirming decisions as the progression of understanding and embracing the gospel is not always linear or immediate. Remember that contextualization is knowing the word of God and knowing your Indian friend and helping them to see what it looks like for them to follow Jesus in their culture from the moment they say, "I am interested in Jesus."

How do we do this? We can help them in the journey without offering the answers. We can lead them to what Jesus says about a question and help them ask the right questions and wait as they find the answers themselves. When it comes time for them to make a difficult decision, they need to understand and embrace the decision they are making. As we journey with them and share the word of God with them and what it means to be faithful to Christ, there comes a day that your friend will make the decision to remove the amulet or empty their god-shelf or change their name and share with their family why they have done so.

Scenario 1:

Your friend comes to you and says, "My name is Ram, the name of a Hindu god. Do I have to change my name?" or "My name is Muhammed, the name of Islam's prophet. Do I have to change my name?"

One response is to ask more questions than you answer: What will your family think if you change your name? What does the name mean to you? Is changing your name going to help you in your discipleship? Is changing your name going to change your family's impression of your decision? Is it better for your family to know that you honor and value them and that you are still part of the family?

Scenario 2:

A friend on the journey says, "I started praying to Jesus after I go to the temple every day."

You might want to say, "You cannot worship Jesus and other gods." But if they are on the journey to Jesus, you can tell them to start wherever they are. Affirm them in that. Tell them you are glad that they started praying to Jesus. Offer to help them understand who Jesus is so that they can pray to Him better and better show their love for Him. At some point, they will conclude that going to the temple does not feel right anymore.

Scenario 3:

A friend tells you, "I still go to the mosque, but I also believe in Jesus."

Tell them that they can pray to Jesus anywhere. Look at the prayers they recite at the mosque and help them to determine which parts are true alongside believing in Jesus and which parts need to be redeemed.

Scenario 4:

A friend asks, "How do I identify myself? Do I tell my family I am a Christian?" You can help them choose the right language to identify themselves:

· *Yeshu Bhakti*: Disciple of Jesus
· *Yeshu ki Chela*: Disciple of Jesus
· *Yeshu* is my *Ista Devta*: Jesus is the God I have chosen, my personal God.
· *Isa iman er upore dichi* (Bengali): I put my faith in Jesus.

We do this contextualization in conversation with them. We continually help them think through their faith and what it means that they are following Jesus.

Here is a sample conversation:

· "Should I tell my family that I am a Christian?"
· "If you tell your family, what will they think?"
· "They will think I am not loyal and that I have left them."
· "OK, so what is a good way for you to share your commitment to Christ with your family? How will you communicate in a way they can understand?"

New followers who came to their own decision and understand what they are doing rarely fall way. Look for answers with your friend. Do not give answers.

Let the Holy Spirit do His job. He is our guide. He will show each person their essentials. We cannot know someone else's essentials as there is no rule that covers the broad scope of Indian views.

Are there any essentials in following Jesus? When you are walking with your friend who is processing what is essential to following Jesus, are changing one's idol worship, amulets, names, and/or intimate relationships essential?

A young lady came from Hindu roots and had been given the name Krishna. Now a believer, she was marrying a man from south India who was generationally Christian. His family would not let their son marry her until she went to the court to officially change her name. Meanwhile, a pastor at the church also has the name Krishna. She did not change her name, so that when people say that Krishna is speaking, Hindu people are willing to visit and hear a Krishna speak. The service is contextualized like a Satsang, and people are very comfortable coming and talking to her.

One of the great things about helping our friends contextualize is that we don't actually do the contextualizing; we help them do it. We know the word of God and we bring the word of God to bear. We primarily help them understand the Word. They know their culture and their community, and we help them understand what it would look like to reveal Christ to their community.

QUESTIONS

As you read through the scenarios, did you find yourself questioning any of them? Take some time to wrestle through those thoughts and questions, asking the Holy Spirit to guide you.

Reflections

CHAPTER TEN

APPROACHES TO SHARING THE GOSPEL

I've been sharing with my team about how creativity is the movement from chaos to order. I was chatting with a young Indian man who was telling me about how people want to hear stories about the chaos around us and how messy the world is. I said, "Think of a piano and its keys. If you plunk them in random order or throw them all on the floor, it's just chaos. If you take all the letters of the alphabet in liquid form and pour them into a bucket, it's chaos. It's in the ordering of things that beauty is shown and creativity happens. You're sitting in this room and everything you look at is something that someone created. All these things around us were made by someone who creatively thought about making something. Look at my blue vase. Someone thought, designed, and painted that vase. If I pick up that vase and smash it on the floor, does the chaos come from the person who made the vase or the person who decided to misuse the vase?" He looked at me and said, "I don't think I want to talk about this anymore." Then he started to laugh. I said, "I know. It's okay." Working with these secular peoples is very different than working with people who are strongly Muslim or Hindu. But more and more of this younger generation, the under 35s, are totally disillusioned with Hinduism and Islam. They lean more Buddhist in some things because they like the idea of emptying their brain of Instagram and other filler.

When ministering to Indians it is important to be flexible and to be in tune with the Holy Spirit. By taking time to listen to your Indian friend, you will have an idea of what they believe, and as you listen to your friend's heart, you will find a story or an idea from the word of God that suits them and their situation. Follow the Holy Spirit and be in tune with open-minded moments. There is no need to charge in and push into the battle. Sharing the gospel is more like a dance.

There are a few Bible stories that can help you process how to approach and share the gospel with your Indian friend. These stories are not one-size-fits-all. You have to weave stories into contexts that are appropriate.

Naaman the Leper
2 Kings 5

Naaman was a general in the Syrian army who had leprosy. His wife had a Jewish servant girl who told her mistress about a prophet in Samaria that could cure Naaman's leprosy if he would visit him. Naaman asked the king to send him to Israel to see the prophet, and the king of Syria wrote a letter to the king of Israel saying, "Heal my servant."

Now the king of Israel, upon reading this letter, was beside himself, but the prophet Elisha sent him a message and said, "Why are you so distressed? Have the man come to me."

Naaman arrived at the tent of Elisha, and Elisha sent word for Naaman to dip in the river Jordan. "That second-rate river?" scoffed Naaman. "Why would I do that?" But his servants said, "If he told you to do something hard, you would have done it, so because he asks this simple thing, why don't you just do it?" So Naaman went to the river, dipped in it, and was healed!

He went back to Elisha and made this faith statement: "Now I know that there is no God in all the world except in Israel." He essentially said, "Now I believe." This would be the equivalent of your Indian friend saying, "Now I believe that Jesus Christ the only true God. He is the Savior."

After this, Naaman made a worship statement. He asked for a load of dirt to build an altar because he was now determined to only worship the God of Israel and none of the gods that the king of Syria worshiped. He said, "I'm never going to worship any other god because I now worship and know the one true God."

Still, Naaman faced a challenge, and he said to Elisha, "Forgive me this thing. When the king goes into the temple of his god, he is old and can't kneel. One of my jobs as the general is to put my arm around him and kneel in the temple." Elisha said, "Go in peace."

That is a powerful statement. Elisha was not giving Naaman permission to worship other gods *and* to worship God. The question Naaman was asking was: Does God understand authority? Naaman was a person under authority and the king he served worshiped other gods. Naaman was asking: Do I have to leave my job now because I work in a place where they worship idols? Elisha's answer was: "No, go in peace." Go, God understands authority.

Your Hindu Indian friend may ask you something like this: "In my house the whole family kneels and worships at the altar every night. What do I do? I committed to believing that Jesus is the only way. Do I need to leave my house?" The amazing answer here is: God understands authority.

As we talk about contextualization of the gospel, we must understand that this is a difficult issue. It is easy for a Westerner in an individualistic society where we make our own decisions. But our Indian friends make decisions in community. They don't have the same authority over their lives that Westerners have. They will need a space to process what it means to be a fully committed follower of Christ as they live with others who are not fully committed to Christ. How do they as a follower of Christ remain true to Him and His word, faithful in worship only to Him, and do that in a loving and kind manner? How do we help them walk that out? Our place is to help our Indian friends go back and live out their faith in a way that their family and friends see Jesus and come to the knowledge of who He is.

I tell my friends this: You can always choose who you worship, and you can always choose what you believe, but you can't always choose where you go. If you are a person under authority, and your parents say that the family is going to the temple today and you don't have a choice as a minor, you can choose who you worship and what you believe, but you don't always choose where you go. If you live in a house where your parents worship idols, you have no authority to throw the idols out of the house. You do have the authority to choose if you worship them or not.

Samaritan Woman at the Well
John 4

As Jesus was sharing with the Samaritan woman at the well, she asked a question: "Our ancestors worshiped on this mountain, but you Jews claim that the place where we must worship is in Jerusalem" (John 4:20). It reads like a statement, but she was asking a question. She may have been trying to distract Jesus, but this was, in fact, a very real question from this Samaritan woman (maybe an Indian woman in our context). Her question was: "This is the place where we worship, and that's the place your people worship. Do I have to leave my place and come to your place to worship? Do I have to stop being a Samaritan and become a

Jew in order to follow You?" Your Indian friend might ask: "Do I have stop being an Indian and become a Westerner? Do I have to leave my culture and people in order to worship Jesus?" That is the question on the table.

Jesus' answer is phenomenal. He said, "A time is coming when you will worship the Father neither on this mountain nor in Jerusalem…. Yet a time is coming and has now come when the true worshipers will worship the Father in the Spirit and in truth, for they are the kind of worshipers the Father seeks" (vv. 21, 23). Jesus' answer was, "No, neither your mountain nor our mountain." For true worshipers it doesn't matter where we sit. It doesn't matter if we sit in a church or in a home, on a mountain in India or near a lake in America. We can remain who we are and where we are as long as we worship in spirit and in truth. This is about a change of heart. It is not a matter of changing dress or outward appearance or a matter of changing worship style. It is a matter of allowing God to change our hearts and give us new life.

This is important because Indians, when they hear the gospel, hear us asking them to become like us, to become a Westerner, to follow the religion of another people. That is what they hear. Perhaps they are interested in following Jesus, and they want to do it, so they ask, "Do I leave my mountain now? Do I leave my home and people now?" Jesus says, "No, you need to stay."

Recall the healed demoniac in Mark 5 who begged to go with Jesus, and Jesus did not let him. He said, "Go home to your own people and tell them how much the Lord has done for you, and how he has had mercy on you" (v. 19). That is what we want—people remaining in their homes and in their community sharing the hope of Christ right where they are. The goal is that they are not kicked out of their context or community.

This is the end goal of contextualization: to bring the gospel in such a way that Indians remain Indians who love Jesus and remain attached to their family and community so they can share the hope they have.

For the Samaritan woman, she went back and told the village. The whole village came to Jesus because they heard the message that she met a Jewish man who said they didn't have to become Jews, that they could meet Him right here right now and follow Him just as they were. What a powerful message that brought a whole community to Christ! Likewise, we must think in terms of winning whole communities, not just one person. We want to see the gospel flow through inter-connected communities, to see a web of influence connected to Christ.

The Early Church
Acts 6 & 10

Controversy in the early church revolved around issues of who was included. The disciples did not hear the conversation Jesus had with the Samaritan woman. They did not hear him say that Samaritans did not have to become Jews to worship Him. So, in the early days of the church they were not yet sure how far the gospel could go.

Acts 6 shows us the first controversy in the church in which the Hebrew believers and the Hellenist believers got into a fight. The Hebrew believers showed partiality among themselves. They believed that to be a true follower of Christ meant one had to be a Hebrew believer. A Hebrew believer was one that followed the old ways: mainline Jews that spoke Hebrew and followed Jewish culture. As a result, the Hebrew believers were not sharing the church's distribution with the Hellenist believers. The Hellenists were Jews that integrated with Greek society. They were ethnic Jews that spoke Greek and followed Greek culture. The Hebrews believers excluded them because they believed that to be a real follower of Christ, to do it right, one had to be a true Jew in culture and language. The early church had to deal with this, so the Twelve gathered all the disciples together and said, "Choose seven men to handle this responsibility." They appointed deacons to make sure that every believer was treated equal in Christ.

The next controversy begins in Acts 10. Peter sat with a man named Cornelius who was a non-Jewish person. Peter shared the gospel and Cornelius and his whole house came to faith. Immediately the council called Peter in and said, "You broke the law and customs. What are you doing with Gentiles?" Peter told the story of how God led him there, how God poured His Spirit out on Cornelius and his house, and how the disciples baptized them.

Then, in Acts 11:18, they have an amazing revelation: "So then, even to the Gentiles God has granted repentance that leads to life." We take this for granted, but the early church was not even sure that Gentiles could be saved. At first, they were not sure about Hellenists, which means they did not think it was true for Gentiles. But here they came to the realization that Gentiles can be saved.

Your Indian friends can be saved. The gospel is not just for Anglo-Saxon Americans. The gospel is for all of us.

The Early Church
Acts 15

Another controversy for the early church was circumcision and the law. The early church agreed Gentiles can be saved, but some among them said that Gentiles must be circumcised and follow the law and tradition. They must become like Jews. The early church leaders ran through it again and Peter ended by saying: "We believe it is through the grace of our Lord Jesus Christ that we are saved, just as they are" (Acts 15:11).

This was another revelation for the early church, and something else we take for granted. The same grace that saved us is the same grace that will save our Indian friends. Listen to what James says: "It is my judgment, therefore, that we should not make it difficult for the Gentiles who are turning to God" (v. 19).

Let this phrase sit in your mind: Don't make life difficult. When discipling someone, is one of your first directives "don't make life difficult"? Our typical starting point is that our friend just needs to do what the Bible says. In this story the apostles are not disregarding truth. Rather, as the grace of God worked among them, their priority became: We are not trying to make your life more difficult than it needs to be.

> As I share the gospel with my Hindu neighbor, the Bible
> tells me to think through what I am sharing with this
> person and how it will affect their life. If my Hindu friend
> accepts Christ, and I tell them to go home, tell their family
> they became a Christian, throw all the idols out of the
> house, and then come and follow Jesus, I have just made
> their lives very difficult. That's not the goal. The goal is to
> help them follow Christ unimpeded and to walk with Him
> every day on a step-by-step journey of faithfulness to Him.

The early church then listed four things that would make following Jesus difficult. The first two were cultural issues: do not eat blood and do not eat animals that were strangled. The apostles and elders were saying, when we share a meal in which Jews and Gentiles are present, for the sake of unity, do not bring these types of food.

In the same way, for the sake of unity with our new Indian friends who visit our homes, we will not have beef and pork at our meals. When you eat together at a restaurant, skip the beef and pork so they can feel comfortable eating with you. Beef and pork are not evil, but it is a simple concession to not make life more difficult for your friends.

> *I won't meet my Hindu Indian friend at a restaurant and order a steak, because my friend has to return home and tell his family that he ate out with a friend. His family will ask, "What did your friend eat?" He will have to answer, "He ate steak." It becomes a problem at that moment. His family will say, "That person is corrupting you." I want to avoid that. I do not want to make his life more difficult.*

The second two issues concerned morality: no sexual immorality and no idolatry. Gentile believers were struggling in the early days of the church. Sexual immorality and idolatry were rampant in the world at that time. By drawing attention to these two issues, the apostles and elders were not saying that it was okay to commit other crimes like theft and murder. They were merely offering a starting point with these two prominent moral issues of the day. They did not burden Gentile believers with the full weight of the law.

> *A friend came to Christ and continued to wear all his rings and amulets that symbolized protection and safety, and he still had idols in his house. For a year he went to church every Sunday and attended small group. The pastor of the church never said anything about it and never asked him to remove his rings. He never questioned him about the rings but continued to walk closely with my friend as he grew deeper in his relationship with Jesus. And then, after one year, my friend decided not to wear them anymore because Jesus' love and protection had truly become all he needed.*

Your Indian friends may have other starting points as well. One is to only worship Jesus. A second is forgiveness as revenge is deeply embedded in Indian culture. No matter the starting point, simply start the journey from the idea of not making their life more difficult.

THOUGHTS

Brainstorm ideas of places you can visit in your community to meet Indians and practice neighborliness and/or write down thoughts that stick out to you from this chapter.

Reflections

PART FOUR

DISCIPLE-ING YOUR INDIAN FRIEND

CHAPTER ELEVEN

DISCIPLESHIP FLOWS FROM THE TABLE

Discipleship is nothing separate from what has already been discussed. It is not a class or curriculum. It is not knowledge we simply pass on.

When discipling your Indian friend, remember that everything flows from the table and from relationship. Our Indian friends desire to be in relationship. Make sure when your friend starts the journey to Jesus, you do not divorce the journey from the relationship you already have. Discipleship flows from the table just like sharing your life flows from the table.

The Larger View of Discipleship

The question we are answering when we are discipling is: What does it look like to follow Jesus? It's true in the West and it's true in India. We could boil discipleship down to making sure that people know facts about Jesus and the Bible, but that is just one small part of discipleship.

The larger view of discipleship is: What does it look like to follow Jesus in this world? How do you treat your spouse now that you are followers of Christ? How do you interact with your children or your parents? How do you live life as a follower of Christ as a university student? What does it mean to be a better son or daughter who is now reflecting the kingdom of God?

It is almost always true that belonging precedes believing. This means people walk with us as we open our lives and our homes to them. Think of it this way: We are discipling people towards a decision about Jesus. Stop thinking about discipleship as what we do after people decide. Think about discipleship as what we do as people decide to walk this journey to understand who Jesus is or as they start in the journey to see where it takes them. We disciple people toward their decision. We allow them to see what it looks like to be a dedicated follower of Christ. We are not just transferring knowledge. We are walking out the command of Christ in which discipleship begins with: "Come and see the goodness of Christ." Everything continues to flow from the table in discipleship.

> *I often refer to the story from Luke 24 in which the disciples were walking on the road to Emmaus. Jesus appeared and began walking with them. They proceeded to tell Him all that they knew about the resurrection. He, in turn, explained the whole Old Testament and everything concerning Himself. Between them all was this incredible exchange of information, but it was still not enough to open the disciples' eyes. It was not until they arrived at their house, sat down at the table, and Jesus broke the bread. Then their eyes were opened. Everything made sense as they sat at the table.*

Discipleship allows people to go on the journey with us. Paul writes to Timothy: "And the things you have heard me say in the presence of many witnesses entrust to reliable people who will also be qualified to teach others. Join with me in suffering, like a good soldier of Christ Jesus" (2 Timothy 2:2–3). Discipleship is not primarily done in a class. If you want to teach someone how to witness, take them with you when you witness. If you want to teach someone what it means to be a good neighbor, take them with you when you are cutting the neighbor's grass. Always have people with you on the journey.

> *I started the journey with several Indians when they were young in faith. We walked to villages together. We walked to the gym together. We sat with people and had tea together. Today, not only do they carry the passion, but*

they have gone a step beyond. Jesus said, "They will do
even greater things then these" (John 14:12). I have seen
the greater things that they actually do because they have
taken what they could from me and have continued in the
journey and taken more from Christ.

We help people in discipleship. They need to hear us say it and see us do it. They need to join us on the journey. Again, discipleship is not just transferring knowledge; it's allowing them to see, hear, and experience it with us. Back to 2 Timothy 2: "And the things you have heard me say in the presence of many witnesses entrust to reliable people who will also be qualified to teach others" (v. 2). See the generations here: Paul is writing to his disciple Timothy about Timothy's disciples (the "reliable people") who will go on a journey with their disciples ("others"). There are four generations of believers in this one passage of Scripture. That is what we long for and are looking for: generations of disciples.

When I worked in Laos, we were discipling young believers
who were in difficult situations. All of them had come
from Buddhist homes and many of them faced real
persecution. If they went out and actively shared their
faith, they might end up in prison. I was praying about
this one day and the Lord gave me a simple phrase: Every
year, every disciple makes one disciple. A simple phrase,
but powerful. I started that with 15 people and over the
next 10 years, I know of over 2,000 people in faith today.
It started with every disciple of the 15 deciding every year
to make at least one disciple. Many of those early disciples
learned that in some years they would make more than

one disciple, which is great, but they set it as a goal to make at least one disciple.

Discipling Friends to Stay

If we are true followers of Jesus, there will be fruit in our lives, and that fruit will bear other fruit (John 15). Within the fruit of our lives is the seed of the gospel, and that seed is planted and bears fruit in the lives of others. It is true for us, and it is true for our disciples.

We see this in the story of the demoniac of the Gadarenes (Mark 5:1–20). Jesus set this man free, and he desired to leave with Jesus. The man begged Him: "Jesus, let me go with You because all the things that led to my demon possession are still right here, and if I stay here, there's a good chance I go back." Jesus' advice to him: "You don't have to worry. You just need to go tell people what I have done for you. I will be with you always." That is the word of Christ to all His disciples, both new and old: I will be with you wherever you go and share your faith, even to the end of the age.

We must guard against separating people from their society. We need to learn to disciple people in their context. If you pull people from their context, far from their people, it will be hard for them to return. Our tendency is to guard a new believer from a home that worships idols or from certain lifestyle choices with their friends, both of which could pull them back to their old ways. We feel protective and want to separate them for a season to make them strong so that one day they can go back. The challenge is, once they are separated, it is incredibly hard to reintegrate. Their people may not accept them or even want them back. We must trust that the God who saved them, the Spirit of God who set them free, and the Christ who gave them salvation is with them in their parents' home and among their friends. The Spirit of God that saved them is the Spirit of God that will keep them and make them strong. This was what Jesus asked of the former demoniac—to stay.

Discipling people to stay means that we will need to be even closer to them. We need to open our house or have a space for them to come if they would like to spend a few hours in prayer before they return home. It means we stand close beside them as they live out their faith in the world. We keep our homes open. If they need to pray every morning, we are there for them. If they need an encouraging word every night, we are there for them. Stand with them to help them stay connected to their community.

Consider the Samaritan woman at the well in John 4. Jesus shared with her, and she immediately went and told the people, "Come and meet this man that told me everything I've ever done" (v. 29). She brought people to Jesus. That is what we encourage our friends to do. They do not have to bring these people to our houses; they just need to introduce them to Jesus and bring them to the family of God. We do not need them to bring people back to us. That is not what Paul told Timothy. He told Timothy to do the work with the reliable ones so they could go and do the work with others. We empower disciples with that same Spirit of Christ that empowers us.

The goal is never to make a disciple. The goal is to make disciples who feel the freedom, empowerment, and desire to go out and make other disciples. If we have disciples with a chief interest in simply going to heaven and being with Jesus, we have not discipled correctly. If we have disciples with a chief interest in seeing all their family, friends, community, and nation join them in the journey, we have created disciples that make disciples. We want friendship that turns into leadership as we continue our ongoing deep discipling friendships and empower them to go out and lead others to Jesus.

Begin With the End in Mind

There are millions of believers in Iran, a country much more difficult than India. The second fastest growing church in the world is in Afghanistan. Not long ago, we had Afghani refugees coming into India, and in a matter of days we found four pastors of over 500 Afghani believers. They did not have one church building or Bible school. They were disciples making disciples, reaching, discipling, and empowering people to do the work of the Spirit. In the West Bank there is a discipleship movement with over 40,000 known believers from a Muslim background. That is a real movement.

If it can happen in the West Bank, Iran, and Afghanistan, it can happen in India. It can start with your Indian neighbor. We never know who the apostle among us will be. You never know if it's the person you are discipling. We are working to see a church planting movement—communities of faith planting to the third and fourth generation of new believers that are raising up leaders and empowering them to see the kingdom of God established from house to house.

This discipleship journey of disciples making disciples is not a pointless endeavor. It has a purpose. If we decide to plant a garden, do we aimlessly and pointlessly drop random seeds in the ground? No, we start with an end in mind. What kind of garden do we want? A flower garden or vegetable garden? We then purchase the correct seeds or plants, and prepare the soil and irrigation, and then we start planting. If we begin with the end in mind, we can more clearly work backwards to the first thing—how we disciple our Indians friend to stay who then disciple more Indians to stay who disciple more Indians, and so on.

So, what do we want to see? We want to see a movement of faith communities in every unreached people group in India. When we look in the eyes of the Indian disciples we are making, we are not thinking about how to make them strong in the

Lord. We look at them and think how they might be a part of a movement starting among their people. How might it be that one day this Indian neighbor returns and reaches people in their village and community and disciples them so that one day a movement to Jesus starts there. We are not just talking a couple disciples here and there, but a movement of people to Christ—hundreds and thousands of disciples gathering around the Lordship of Christ.

If you don't have church planting movement, you need to start your first church (a gathering of disciples). This movement is not about church buildings. It is about a movement in which communities of people who follow Jesus are created in an unreached context. A church is a Christ-centered community or gathering of disciples that meets on a regular basis for the purpose of growth, encouragement, and Christlikeness. It is disciples gathered, empowered, and released to go. In the disciples' DNA they understand that we have one gathering today, but every person in that gathering needs to be a part of seeing the kingdom of God grow. The end in mind is people meeting together in communities in which those communities make it easier to build more communities.

If you don't have church, you make your first disciple. With this book, we are looking for those first disciples. We do not disciple them toward knowledge, but toward action, asking what it means to be a follower of Christ. Disciple your disciple to go and make other disciples and reflect the kingdom of God and the character and nature of Christ. We also disciple them towards creating a gathering that produces other gatherings. Here we have a few disciples on the journey and we organize them into communities, making disciples that recognize others who are part of the family. They begin to know who is in the family and they always leave space at the table for one more person who would like to join.

I have a writers group in my life, and I see the day when this group is looking at the Sermon on the Mount. I see writers responding to beatitudes and artists painting about beatitudes, and all of them coming back the next week to share how it relates to their lives. I see poets and songwriters and a whole creative community of people interacting around the Word. They may all be at different places in their journey with Jesus and one's interaction with the Word might be more like a stick man while another who is further along interacts more like a Picasso, but they are sharing with each other, and the young ones on the journey grow as the older ones move forward. I can visualize deep and broad life impact but must start small and grow.

If you don't have a disciple, then you look for the deep, meaningful relationship and share your life and the gospel with those friends. As you take the journey, keep the end in mind. This is not about that one person coming to Christ, but about what you are doing today to prepare this person to become a person God can use to establish His kingdom. We are not pointing them towards individualism. They do not accept Jesus so they can simply go to heaven, but they accept Jesus to be a part of establishing His kingdom right here and now on the earth among all their people. They are the first fruits of the gospel for their people.

God has plan and purpose for their life, but it's not just for them to be saved or be a part of a church, but to use them to establish His church among their people. So, make sure when you are discipling people, disciple them with a broader perspective. Christ wants to establish His kingdom among all the peoples of India. That is why we are discipling them. That's why Christ is calling them.

QUESTIONS

What did your discipleship journey look like? How was it similar or different to the way that discipleship is done in the Bible and in India?

Is there anyone in your life that you feel the Lord asking you to walk alongside more intentionally, in a discipleship type way? If so, what is a practical step you can take this week to start that journey?

Reflections

CHAPTER TWELVE

DISCIPLESHIP FLOWS FROM A CHRIST-CENTERED GOSPEL

*One evening our team looked at the story of the
Samaritan woman at the well (John 4), and it appeared
to us that there was a sense of competitiveness in the
story: you're different than me because of this. The story
even starts with the Pharisees comparing how many
people John the Baptist and Jesus had baptized. When
we are man-centered, we look at the things that divide
us and make us different from each other. But "from
one man he has made all the nations, that they should
inhabit the whole earth" (Acts 17:26). When we get into
the discussions that only look at what separates us rather
than at what brings us together, that is a man-centered
gospel, not a Jesus-centered gospel. The Samaritan
woman brings up all the differences between them, and
Jesus says, "I am the Messiah, the one you have been
looking for." And suddenly He becomes the center
of the story.*

With all we have discussed so far, we now take a step back to say: *This all
flows from a Christ-centered gospel.* Our discipleship flows from a Christ-centered
gospel. Discipleship begins with people who have only said that Jesus sounds interesting and that they want to know more, so remember, we are discipling our
friends toward a decision.

The Christ-centered gospel announces that Jesus is the Christ, David's son,
Israel's King, thus the Son of God (see John 1:49); that He reigns, having resurrected from death, and now reconciles people to God; therefore, all nations should
repent and believe.

Anything less than this is not the whole gospel.

And the goal of the gospel is much further than we often describe it. It is not just that Jesus died for you. It is not just that Jesus saves. The goal of the gospel is the glory of God. In 1 Timothy 1:11, the gospel is called "the gospel of the glory of the blessed God" and in 2 Corinthians 4:4, "the gospel of the glory of Christ." The goal of the gospel is God receiving the glory due His name by all nations, tribes, and tongues giving worship and honor. It is in the glorification of God that people receive the fullness of life. In the honoring of God people come into the fullness of their humanity for which God created them. The gospel above all aims to show the worth and greatness of God, and therefore, the gospel must be Christ-centered.

As we share the gospel, we are not sharing a man-centered gospel; we are sharing a Christ-centered gospel. The book of Genesis does not start with sin but with the greatness of God. In the beginning God created everything out of Himself. He created all things, and they were all good. He breathed life into us and created us to be with Him. It is only in the context of this great God that the weight of sin can be understood. Genesis chapter 3 only makes sense when we understand who this God is that we are sinning against.

The Four Questions

Preaching the Christ-centered gospel requires that we answer four questions:

1. Who is Christ?
2. What has Christ done?
3. Why is Christ important?
4. How should we respond?

Often our gospel presentation only includes "what has Christ done" and "how should we respond." We skip the other two, but all four are crucial in sharing a Christ-centered gospel with Indians. Let's unpack these four questions:

Who is Christ?

Repentance makes zero sense until our Indian friends understand a good, all powerful, loving God. You cannot move to point B until your disciple understands point A. If you ask your Muslim friend who God is, they may say that He is judge. If you ask your Buddhist friend who God is, they will likely say they are not sure there even is a God. Ask your Hindu friend and they will say there are many gods who act and express themselves differently. Ask your philosophical Hindu friend and they may say that everyone is a representation of brahman and so we are all God. If God is one of many gods or if He is just a vindictive judge, then repentance has no meaning.

Oftentimes, we preach the gospel and include a "you need to repent," but the question here is, "Who am I repenting to and why?" Repentance only makes sense in the context of fully understanding who God is. So, who is Christ? What differentiates this God from the gods they worship now? What is unique about this God? God through Christ reigns over the nations. He is the Creator, King, Ruler, Sustainer, the God of Abraham, Isaac, and Jacob. He comes from a historical context—God is the God who works in history. For the gospel presentation to make sense, it must begin with who is God.

What has Christ done?

In our gospel presentations in the West, we typically start here because we commonly share with people who are like us or people who know something about who Christ is. They have probably heard the story of Jesus, that He lived on this earth, He healed and performed miracles, He died for our sins, and God resurrected Him from the dead. In the West, we tell someone what Christ has done for them and we say, "Jesus died for you," it's likely that person will understand our meaning.

But with your Indian friends, particularly those who are Hindu, if you start with what Christ has done and tell your friend that Jesus died for them, they may find that problematic, or at the very least confusing. Because Hindus believe in karma. If you tell your Hindu friend that Jesus died this horrible death, they might think, "Oh, man! What did he do in his past life? He must have been paying for some really bad stuff." Because everyone pays for their own karma; no one can pay for someone else's karma.

Statements that we see as irrefutable can become statements of misunderstanding if we skip that first question and our friends do not know who Christ is. Only in understanding Christ as the perfect one without sin and as one who needs no redemption can they understand His death as a perfect sacrifice, untainted with the weight of sin and karma.

Why is Christ important?

Your Indian friend may say, "Okay, He created all of this and has done this great thing, but what does that mean to me? How does that impact my life? I have many gods, so why is this one important?"

Remember that our societies are different. Western society is a legal society. Eastern society is a relational society. In the West redemption matters more, while in the East reconciliation matters more.

At the heart of their journey every Indian seeks answers this thing that matters most to them: We can be reconciled to God. Jesus is important for your friend because through Christ God reconciles humanity's relationship with Himself, with each other, and with the world. Christ is the one that God sent to reconcile us to Himself; that is why He is important.

How should we respond?

Let's take this final question by looking at a message from the Apostle Paul in Acts 17. We'll see the use of the other three questions in this story as well. This passage is a good model for preaching a Christ-centered gospel.

This is the only recorded message in Acts that was directed strictly to a Gentile audience. Most other messages in Acts were directed towards a Jewish audience, and when dealing with a Jewish audience Paul often quoted the Old Testament because he was talking to an audience that understood Old Testament language. In Acts 17, we have a message directed to a Gentile, non-Jewish audience. We know that Paul was known for lengthy discourse. The author Luke has given us the highlights of a rich message that would have gone much deeper into the topic.

Beginning in verse 22, "Paul then stood up in the meeting of the Areopagus and said: 'People of Athens! I see that in every way you are very religious.'"

At the start Paul affirmed his audience. This is not how we typically deal with idolatry, is it? Usually when we see an idol, we ask, "Why are you worshipping that idol? Don't you know idols are dead? They're demonic!" That is our typical starting point.

> I have a story that didn't go well. It went very contrary to my expectations, but God was still gracious to work it out somehow. When I first came to faith, I was trying to explain to my sister that these gods she follows are demons. We were at a restaurant, and we got very loud. She was so angry with me. Thankfully, there were so many things happening in her life that she later forgot the actual conversation and let it go. But the idea of idols and demons stuck with her. I learned the lesson the hard way. Don't do that. It goes badly.

Here Paul found good even in idol worship. He did not affirm idol worship, but he affirmed their searching hearts. Essentially, he said, "I see that you are seekers. You are the kind of people that have longing in your hearts. I am here to affirm you, not condemn you." Our response is to be the kind of people that can look for the good and speak affirming words of life over people, and not start with words of death.

> I have had many moments of people bringing me to their god-shelf and showing me which ones they follow and why. We have rich conversations with that as a starting point.
>
> My mom has become friends with an Indian family in the States. The first time I visited I was helping in the kitchen when the mother took me to her god-shelf to show me which ones she follows and why. This was just the beginning of a relationship so I felt no pressure to pull out a Paul moment and say, "Well, this is who you are actually searching for." I just honored her devotion and was respectful knowing that opportunities will come in our relationship. And as I have honored and respected her beliefs, she will most likely do the same when I share my beliefs about the God I follow and why.

You don't have to share it all at once. When someone talks to you about what they believe, honor that. It's not saying you agree with it, but you can be respectful of their beliefs.

To verse 23, "for as I walked around and looked carefully at your objects of worship, I even found an altar with this inscription: to an unknown god. So you are ignorant of the very thing you worship—and this is what I am going to proclaim to you."

There is a historical story behind this comment by Paul. This story of the unknown god is in ancient Greek literature, and Paul encountered this story somewhere. There was a time of disease in the city of Athens, and they tried everything to keep the disease from spreading but people kept dying. The people prayed to every god at every temple in the city and nothing happened. One day someone said, "Maybe there is a god we missed, one we don't know yet." They released a goat to see where it went, and the goat went to a spot and stopped. They sacrificed the goat and the plague stopped, so they built an altar there to a god they did not know who was able to stop the plague.

Paul walked in and said, "What you have been ignorantly worshipping I am now proclaiming to you." Their ears perked up.

> We celebrated Rabindranath Tagore's birthday (it's a national holiday in India), and we decided to honor him and his writing at our writers group. He was a prolific and amazing writer. I gave some of his writings to two of our interns and asked them to find something that resonated with them. I asked them to share their response at the writers group. One of them wrote an amazing, powerful response. Then when reading this scripture, the interns connected the dots. They said, "It's like Paul was studying the history and poets of the society and the culture so he would know what to say to them." Yes, that's exactly what he did. This passage affirms those who are writers, creatives, and deep thinkers. I have heard that Tagore wrote an essay or poem about Jesus every Christmas. Amazing that there is a space in Bengali culture to honor the place that Jesus holds.

Throughout this study we have been talking about knowing the people we are communicating with. Paul knew his audience. We need to spend time learning their stories and history. Something in the history or the story of a people may very well elicit something in their lives that leads to a deep conversation. Look for that story. God will give you His perfect wisdom to speak into the stories of their lives and to speak into their lives through their stories. Paul knew these people and affirmed them.

Verses 24 and 25, "the God who made the world and everything in it is the Lord of heaven and earth and does not live in temples built by human hands. And he is not served by human hands, as if he needed anything. Rather, he himself gives everyone life and breath and everything else."

Remember the first of our four questions: Who is Christ? He is the Creator of everything. He is the Lord of heaven and earth. He is not confined to a temple or to any space. He does not need human help. He is the Giver of life. See in verses 24 and 25 how Paul is answering the question of the unknown god. They do not know who it is and all the gods they are worshipping have confused them, so Paul gave a clear articulation of who this God is. As we are discipling people, we need to give a clear understanding of who this God is that we are asking them to follow.

In verse 26, "from one man he made all the nations, that they should inhabit the whole earth; and he marked out their appointed times in history and the boundaries of their lands."

Our second question is: What has Christ done? He created all of us, all nations, all people. We were all created by Him. Paul gave us something of the nature of who God is. He told his audience and us one aspect of God: He is the Creator, and you were created by Him. He said to his audience, "I am a Jew, and you are a Gentile. We are from different cities, but we are all the same family. We were all created by God, and you need to know that He is your Father. You need to know that He has a link to you. He is not a foreign or separate God. He is the God who created you." Our Indian friends need to understand that Jesus is not the God of the West but is the God that created them, every Indian, every language group and tribe. He created all of us uniquely for His glory.

Verses 27 to 29, "God did this so that they would seek him and perhaps reach out for him and find him, though he is not far from any one of us. 'For in him we live and move and have our being.' As some of your own poets have said, 'We are his offspring.' Therefore, since we are God's offspring, we should not think that the divine being is like gold or silver or stone—an image made by human design and skill."

Why is Christ important? He is important because God did all of this so that we would seek Him and find Him. Everything God has done is for a purpose. He created us so that we would seek and find Him—and He is not far from anyone of us. We were created in His image, so we cannot think that He is like an idol because we are not idols. We are flesh and blood, and we are spirit, and the God who created us did so in His image. Therefore, God is not a stone or wood. He is important because He made us for the purpose of finding Him and experiencing Him. He made us for the purpose of reveling in His glory.

In verses 30 and 31, "in the past God overlooked such ignorance, but now he commands all people everywhere to repent. For he has set a day when he will judge the world with justice by the man he has appointed. He has given proof of this to everyone by raising him from the dead."

Now we arrive at the answer to the final question of how should we respond to God, the Creator, King, and Ruler of the world, the one who made us in His image, the one who made us in order that we would seek and find Him? We should repent of our old ways and old allegiances, and we should give allegiance to Christ. We should give loyalty to Christ to follow Him. That is what He has called us to do.

We see in this short message how Paul answered our four questions to an audience who knew nothing. Verse 32 says, "When they heard about the resurrection of the dead, some of them sneered, but others said, 'We want to hear you again on this subject.'" That is the power of the gospel.

Sometimes you will share with people, and they say, "No, this is crazy. We worship many gods, and you worship one god. What you're saying makes no sense to me." Not everybody will understand everything that we share about the gospel.

But when we rightly share the gospel, the Spirit of God is working with us, and when the Spirit of God is working with us, it will be like verses 33 and 34 say, "At that, Paul left the Council. Some of the people became followers of Paul and believed." Notice the sequence: Some of them followed Paul and believed. You will find that some friends will belong long before they believe. It is okay that they are following you as long as you are pointing them toward Jesus and toward the glory of God.

> *I was walking with a friend one day and I was trying to convince him about Jesus right there in our first conversation. I think I did a terrible job and I felt like I blew it. I apologized to the Holy Spirit. I said, "God, I am so sorry. I'm terrible at this. I'm messing it up. I feel like I am getting in Your way." The Holy Spirit whispered to me, "I put you in this for relationship. Seed is scattered everywhere in every way, but discipleship happens through relationship, just like this conversation will move forward through relationship." It reminded me that so often I want to win the argument or convince somebody. I want them to believe right away. But what the Spirit said to me was exactly what happened. It was months of more visits, more talks, and more prayer.*

We can be hard on ourselves because we want this for our friends. Give yourself time. You do not have to win the argument. You do not have to convince someone right away or every time. At times, you do not even have to have the last word. God has put you in that relationship and He will reveal Himself as you share the gospel. Always encourage and invite people to journey with you, that is what discipleship is.

You do not have to share all four of these questions at once. The most important thing is to make sure that you are fully sharing all of these things in the context of your relationship. Make sure they have a good understanding of who Christ is. Make sure they know the beautiful and incredible things Christ has done for us. Make sure they know why He is so important. Then what you will find is that you do not need to present the question of how to respond because you find their response will be, "What do I need to do to be saved?" As people reflect on the glory of God and what He has done and why He is important, there is a natural outcome to be made right with God and walk with Him.

Are They Ready to Be Discipled?

The question is asked: How do I know if my friend is ready to be discipled?

We listen for an invitation and look for any opening of the door. As soon as you see it, walk in.

Their response may be simple: "Wow, that's interesting. I've never heard that before." Invite them: "I do a study nearly every day. If you would like to know more about God and what it means to be His follower, I would love to do that with you over coffee. Anytime you are available, let me know."

Or maybe they tell you they had a vision and want to know more about Jesus. Your response: Dive straight in.

For those who are more reticent and unsure, walk with them in whatever place they are. Meet them at their point of interest.

> *In one city, there were quite a few cracked doors. We just kept pushing on those doors as they opened wider and wider, and continued to share the truth of who Jesus is and allowing Him to do His work in the people's lives.*

Someone once put it this way: Whenever you are with your friend, pretend or imagine that they want to believe in Christ and follow Him—and let them prove otherwise. Sometimes, we enter conversations defensively or try to work the gospel pieces together so perfectly that it all comes out sounding more manufactured than natural. Instead, go into every conversation with the mindset that people want to hear and receive this good news about Jesus.

Remember that your friend may follow before they believe. You are leading them to Jesus and discipling them towards a most precious decision.

QUESTIONS

Can you answer the four questions of preaching a Christ-centered gospel? Take some time to practice answering these with a friend until it feels natural and easy to share.

As you read this section, was there any moment that the gospel came alive to you in a new way? If so, take some time to thank the Lord for that and then share about it with a friend.

Reflections

This is just the start.

You may not think you're ready to take this journey with your Indian friend. Remember the Spirit of God, who has all wisdom and power, is with you. Don't go in fear believing that you don't know enough to engage with your friend. The Holy Spirit is enough. He will give you words you need in the moment.

If you possess an open and humble heart to be a learner and a listener, and if you allow your friend to walk with you in your journey as you walk with Christ, you will be able to lead your friend and disciple them to Jesus.

We disciple people to make disciples. We do not disciple people so they can go to heaven one day. We disciple our Indian friends so they can make disciples that make disciples so that the kingdom of God will be established among Indian people around the world.

About us

This book was compiled by a community of Live Dead team members who live and work in India.

We serve in multi-cultural teams among unreached peoples, engaging them day in and day out with the good news through business platforms.

What's amazing about all of our teams is how each individual works within their strengths and the complementary strengths God has given their team!

- Athletes bring the community together around sports and fitness.
- Artists create together.
- Therapists process life and living with community members.
- Baristas and bakers serve up delicious coffee, tea, and treats as people gather.
- Adventurous hearts trek and climb in remote places.
- Gamers compete and connect online and in-person.

Whatever your giftings and passion are, God can use it and it's likely that you're not alone! Today there is a body of Christ followers in India ready to join with you to release your gifts.

If you're interested in discovering how you can be a greater part, connect with us at eliza@thecommontable.us.

Open your table and join ours

Text "INDIA" to 234-249-3396

You'll receive a text response requesting your email address. Once you text that back, you're at the table with us.

We'll email you the following resources to use your voice and start your journey to India.

1. Join a Pray Band. Receive email and video updates from one of our teams and pray with them.
2. Lead a book study with this book.
3. Come serve with our teams.

Also available from

LIVE | DEAD

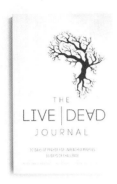

The Live Dead Journal

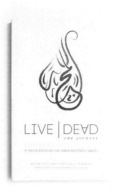

Live Dead The Journey

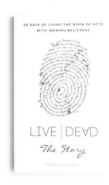

Live Dead The Story

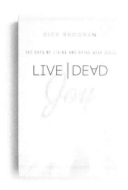

Live Dead Joy

The Live Dead Journal:
Her Heart Speaks

Diario: Vivir Muerto

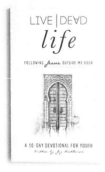

Live Dead Life

Live Dead India:
The Common Table

This Gospel

Leading Muslims to Jesus

Live Dead Together

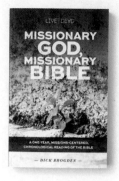

Missionary God, Missionary Bible

Cannibal Island

Hunter and Hunted

Indomitable

Proverbs

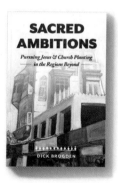

Sacred Ambitions

Check out our full line of Live Dead books at
www.abidepublishers.com which include:

Individual and group devotionals
Graphic novel biographies of missionaries
Challenging and inspiring stories from work among unreached people